THE MAGIC DOLPHIN

Written by Kirsten Hintner

Scientific Adviser Dr Peter Evans

Illustrator Alice Ormiston

PUBLISHED IN 2014 BY CREATIVE CONSERVATION

THE MAGIC DOLPHIN

978-0-9930819-0-3

First Published 2014 by
www.creativeconservation.co.uk

Printed and bound in Great Britain by
www.bookprinting.uk.com
Berforts Information Press

THE MAGIC DOLPHIN

Dear Anna

A gift from us all here at Sea Watch Foundation
to say how grateful we are for all your
wonderfully creative 'Puzzlers'!
We wish you lots of luck in your new job

Viola
x

To all the brilliant adoptees of the dolphins of Cardigan Bay. Many of whom have written diaires about their visits to New Quay, West Wales, which have been a huge inspiration to me. This book is for you all.

My thanks to Dr Peter Evans whose guidance and advice has secured the accuracy of the scientific information given in this book. Although The Magic Dolphin can be enjoyed for its fictional purposes, it can also be confidentially utilised as a strong educational tool. Peter has extensive knowledge of cetaceans and works tirelessly towards research and conservation, to ensure their future remains a safe and healthy one.

Kirsten Hintner

This book is dedicated to my family (my pod), who have remained unwavering in their support and encouragement during the production of The Magic Dolphin. Thank you.

In memory of my grandmother, who would love to have read my book x

Kirsten x

Contents Page

1. A New Arrival

'PLOP'. Opening my eyes I looked around and all I could see was blackness, and all I could feel was cold cold water after the warm warm tummy where I had spent my last twelve months. OOPS. I'd been born and didn't realise it, tail first, then my head coming into a new exciting and rather scary world. But before I had a chance to look around I felt myself being lifted up from underneath. Everything was becoming lighter and brighter as I rose higher. There it was again, another nudge from beneath lifting me higher. Suddenly I was breaking through the cold water and here was a new sensation,

"Oh it's so bright" I squeaked, instantly squeezing my eyes tightly shut.

Next I was aware that I was sucking in warmish air through the top of my head! '*Pschhhhhhhhh*' it went as I felt it enter my body filling me up like a balloon. Before I could adjust to the dazzling brightness and get my bearings I felt myself sinking down again, back into the cold water. On opening my eyes, a large, kindly looking face was peering at me and making clicking noises. This face was joined by another, then three, then four, and very soon I was being checked over and admired by lots of smiling grey faces, all excitedly clicking and clacking at me and at each other.

I was an hour-old, male, bottlenose dolphin and I had been born into a cold, dark watery world. Although it was all very exciting to see so many friendly faces obviously happy that I was there, I longed for the warmth and comfort of my mum's womb. I felt that I had arrived into this new place before I was ready. The dark, cosy nest where I had spent the previous twelve months growing and developing seemed as if it was not available to me anymore. The new noises around me were the ones I was going to have to get used to now. They were all so loud and sharp and *everywhere* compared to the soft, muffled lullabies that had so often coaxed me gently in and out of sleep.

I soon learned that I had a very large family. My mum, whose name I learned was Nic Nic and whose face was the first I had encountered, then my dad, older brother Splash, aunties, uncles and grandparents, too.

I also quickly discovered that I would have to regularly return to the glare of the air-world above to breathe oxygen into my lungs to stay alive. This bright place hurt my eyes terribly and to be honest I only ever wanted to stay for the brief time that was needed to exhale and inhale, and no longer. Anyway, once I had mastered rising up to the surface, with a few helpful up-lifts again from Mum, I began to check myself over.

Most of me was light brown in colour apart from my completely white belly, and some curious pale stripes around my body.

"Your foetal folds" whistled my mum softly, seeing me examining myself. *"When you were growing inside me you lay in a tight little ball. Those white stripes show how your body was bent around itself to allow you to fit in here for all that time"* she explained, nodding towards her stomach.

I was very small, about one metre in length, from my pointed beak down to my tail - *'flukes'* as I was later corrected by Aunt Grace. These flukes seemed to grow out of the end of my body and then separated into two points that I could wave around.

As I began to experiment a little, I discovered that if I very slightly moved my flukes up and down just once or twice, I found myself gliding through the water with incredible ease as the ground passed by underneath. *'Swooooossssh'*, another tail flick and I was off again, flying over stones and soft green areas, this time faster and gliding just a little bit further than before. The harder I swiped my tail through the water, the further I got each time, until… *"OUCH!"*, 'what was that?'

Mum was prodding me hard into my side with her beak and shaking her head at me whilst clicking frantically.

"Your first lesson, my dear, is to stick very close by my side" she snapped, inflicting another prod for good measure. I had a feeling this was going to be the first of many scoldings from Mum.

Stretched out fully, I could see I was long and slim and had two rather soft, floppy things sticking out either side of my body.

'I wonder what possible use these will be for?' I thought as I flapped them pathetically up and down, looking from one to the other.

"Don't you know that all the creatures in the world's oceans would go Cr-aZY for a pair of those!" came a booming voice from above. *"Finely tuned steering instruments is what they are,"* it went on as I tried to manoeuvre myself onto my side so I could look up to where the voice was coming from.

"Tooooo late" came a sing-songy whistle, now from underneath.

Whatever it was, it was finding this very amusing.

"You gotta learn how to swim like a real dolphin", this time coming from right next to me.

"Highly prized pectoral fins is what they are, Sonny, and if you want to do maaaaagic like me" it whistled in whispery tones…

Quickly I spun around determined to catch it but instead saw nothing but open

water, *"then you gotta be quick, and fast, and nippy, and AAAAGILE"* it sang again as the most wonderfully, impressive dolphin floated down in front of me and was now looking me straight in the eyes. It was awesome! Very big and strong and with eyes that twinkled with excitement.

"Oh leave him alone" chirped Mum, swimming over to us, *"Don't tease the poor fella, he'll get there in his own time, he will."* And as I turned back to this wonderful specimen of a dolphin, he had gone, just like that, vanished into the blue. It turned out he was my dad, Rip Torn.

The other part of my body that I discovered at a later stage was a curious dark coloured, triangular lump on my back. It was after seeing these very elegant looking things on the other dolphins that I wondered if I also had one. I hoped so because they looked mightily impressive! They seemed to slice through the water at an alarming rate, making a *'Swishhhhh, Swoshhhhh'* sound as they flew by. I could only gaze in wonderment. It was a dorsal fin. Unfortunately mine, like my pectoral fins, was soft. I knew this because I could feel it flopping about on my back. In others it seemed to be much firmer. *"If I could just see it"*, I muttered. *"If only I could quickly just....spin around fast enough to just.....see it!"* muttering more. *"Maybe if I turn this way instead.... I might catch it if I could spin just a little faster..."* I spluttered as I span around and around in tighter and tighter circles desperately trying to catch a glimpse of my fin. But try as I might, I just couldn't spin quite far or fast enough. All I was doing was chasing my tail and creating such a spectacle of myself that I had gathered quite an audience!

"Oh, just look at my baby brother!" whistled Splash.

"*Heeheeheeheehee, isn't he just adorable*" squeaked Coral, who watched with her mum, Topnotch. "*He looks daft*" chirped another.

"*You'll only see it if you're as fast as me!*" added Splash with a double somersault and figure-of eight-twirl just to impress the gathering crowd.

I had completely exhausted myself out with all the spinning and had nothing to show for it apart from feeling dizzy and making a fool of myself. '*I'll show them*', I thought as I returned to Mum, out of breath and with tail hanging low. '*I'll show them how my dorsal fin can swish and swoosh.*'

2. A Young Visitor

Saturday 19th June

The car is jam packed. I'm crammed into the back, stuck alongside all our suitcases, wash-bags, squashed sandwiches, bottles of juice and my brother who's being a total pain-a-rooney, as usual! Every time I try to write in my notebook, he leans over me pretending to be looking for something, then accidentally nudges my arm so I jerk across the page. Then there's my Dad who thinks he's Lewis blimmin Hamilton, flying around blind bends and hitting EVERY bump without slowing down. I'm sure he's doing it on purpose. There he goes again

Thank goodness they've stopped for a coffee break so I can write properly for 5 mins....

I was just thinking back to the moment when mum gave me the 'surprise' Christmas present. I can even remember how the box felt and the terrible, embarrassing reindeer wrapping paper and huge pink shiny bow! Even though it looked about the right size and shape, I was dreading opening it because I didn't know what to do if it turned out *not* to be what I hoped *it* was. I'd dropped heaps of hints, but sometimes you never know with parents!!

I'd just have to pretend that I loved it, whatever *it* was, and try again next year.

Well, what a relief to see the little dolphin head sticking out of the box, and what an AWESOME pressie.

I asked loads of questions after that – "Where do the dolphins live?" "What do they eat?" "How long have they lived there?" "How old is mine?" "Does she have any family?" And the most important one.......When can we go to see them?"

And just six months later, here we are, on our way to West Wales, to see the dolphins! My dolphin!!! That's if we ever get there in one piece that is.

So, here's where we're off to, if any of you'ssss are interested?? Nice map huh! That's me with the red trousers on by the way.

Uh oh, they're back now... it's back to the scribble again.. Not sure there's much point to this at the moment if none of my friends back home will even be able to read it.

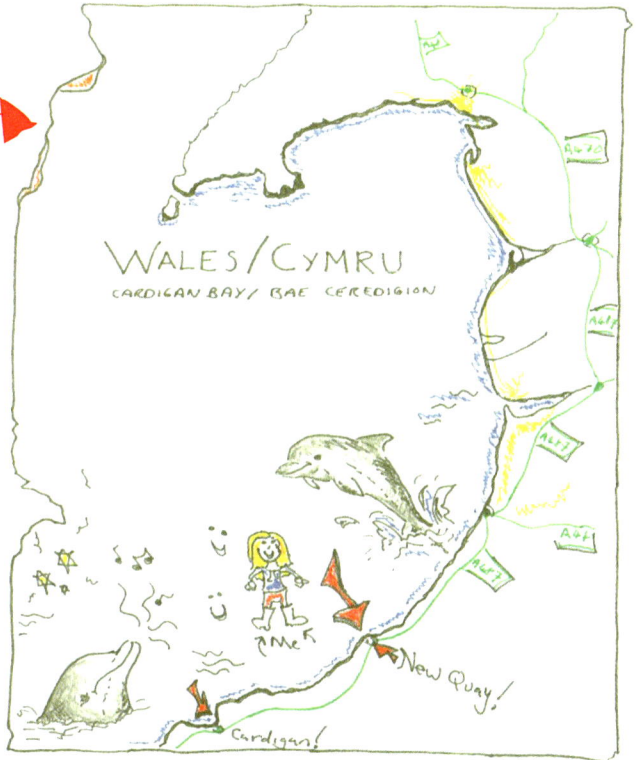

WALES/CYMRU
CARDIGAN BAY/ BAE CEREDIGION

New Quay!

Cardigan!

Parents are completely useless at talking quietly. I can clearly hear them from the back...

Dad's moaning about having to stay in rainy UK for our holiday and going on about hot Spanish sun. Mum's telling him not to be so selfish, and that she has high hopes that coming to see the dolphins might actually help me. To inspire me so I will do better at school. Anything to help!

Oh NO.. she's now going on about my last parent's evening again!!! Dad's face is turning purple. This is def. not gonna end well......gulp!! HELP!

Yeah ok, it wasn't a brilliant idea to crumble Barney's tripe sticks into mum's handbag so that every time she opened it, the person sitting close by started to gag. All my friends said it was 'First class entertainment!!', and can't wait for next year! (BTW, Barney's our gorgeous tan-coloured terrier who had to stay with Aunty Angie whilst we're away because he gets over excited about car journeys), bless :o))

I admit I'm not brilliant at school. I hate maths, can't understand any foreign language, and am useless at chemistry but I do enjoy art, and LOVE writing. That's why I'm keeping this diary — to show people that I am good at something. And I'm going to get 10/10 for it too! You'll see.

Hey!! I can see New Quay and guess what, not a drop of rain in sight, yet!! It looks gorgeous and sunny.

Time for my first 'snappy happy' ;o))))

This summer's gonna be great!

I can't sit still anymore. Jack, my incredibly boring, older brother is glued to his games thingy. He just grunts every now and then. You could explode a bomb right next to him and he wouldn't notice.

16

4pm - Yahooooooo, finally we've arrived! I have a good feeling about this place. This is me, outside the Bed and Breakfast when dad span me around and around. He's still moaning about the rain, even though it isn't raining!

The first thing I noticed about being by the sea were the gulls flying above us. They're very loud. Oh and then the smell of the sea, all salty and sharp, not like the dull and boring air back home. Things even sound different here. I can hear people laughing and chatting on the beach, and the waves on the sand. Also the sound of flip-flops flapping along the cobbly streets.

6.20pm - The view from our rooms at the 'Golygfa Dolffin' (think that's how you spell it) B&B is fab-tab-u-lous!!! *Golygfa Dolfinn'*, is Welsh for *'Dolphin View'*. I know that because of the lady who lives here. She told mum they can see the dolphins sometimes from the rooms and that we won't want to leave. I already don't!

17

Me again, with dad's binoculars. I'm looking for dolphins from our room. I can see the whole town and beach from here. It's perfect! I'm so happy and want to stay forever! I can't wait to get down to the quay and dip my toes into the sea. Bet the water's really cold.

Urgh!! What is that smell?? That is so disgusting. Jack's only gone and hung his rank smelling socks out of the window!

That's the one bad part to this holiday - I HAVE to share a room with HIM! Hope he leaves me alone, and remembers to wash his feet! Last time we were stuck in the same room, his socks were so foul, they went stiff!

9.30pm - OK, back from dinner now. Well stuffed after all that food!

When I adopted Nic Nic, I got some goodies in my pack. One was a booklet telling me all about dolphins...

Amazing Fact: Apparently 53 million years ago, dolphins didn't actually look like dolphins do today. They were called 'Pakicetids' and lived on land!!! But, they drank and hunted from rivers and streams and eventually turned into dolphins. That's very, very weird isn't it!?

forward facing
eyes

— fur

Pakicetid looks nothing like a dolphin! More like a funny-looking hippo to me.

long tail

very small
ears

quite long
limbs

Short hands
and feet
(look hoof-like)

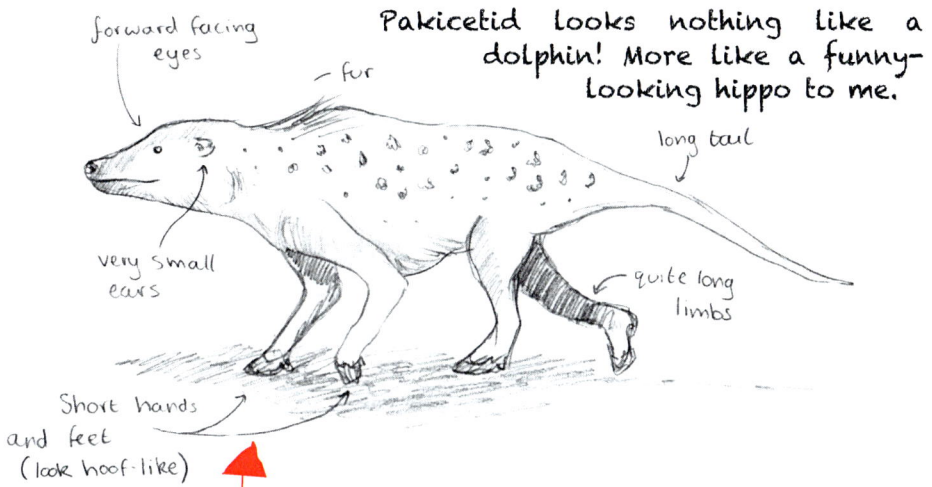

How could this   turn in to this???

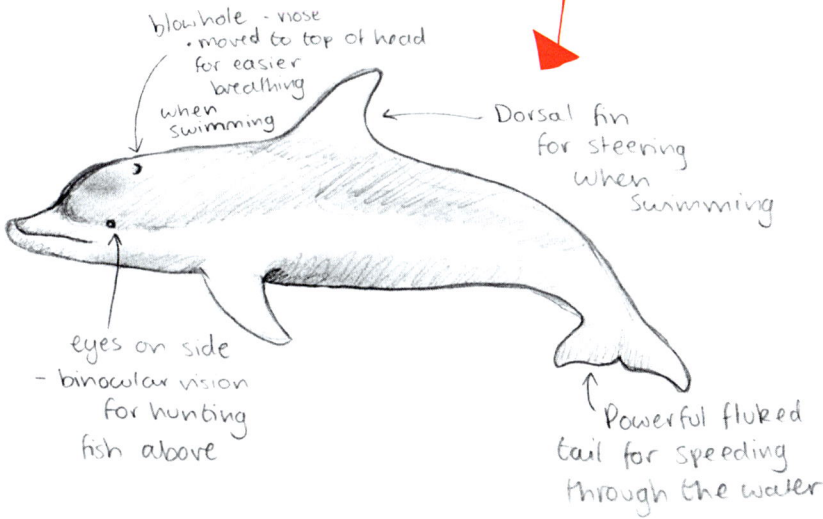

blowhole - nose
· moved to top of head
for easier
breathing
when
swimming

Dorsal fin
for steering
when
swimming

eyes on side
- binocular vision
for hunting
fish above

Powerful fluked
tail for speeding
through the water

As Pakicetids adapted to water their eyes moved to the sides of the head and the nose moved to the top of its head!

I wonder if humans evolved from something else millions and squillions of years ago? I bet Jack evolved from something completely different to the rest of us, like a dung-beetle!

By the way, did you know the blue whale can grow up to 30 metres! WOWZERS!!! And the smallest is the harbour porpoise at 1.5m So cute ;o))))) Just like a baby dolphin!

CUTIE PIE OR WHAT XXX

My favourites are still the bottlenose dolphins though. They always look so friendly and smiley. They are also very, very smart.

Wow, suddenly feel very tired. All this studying must be wearing me out. Off to Bedfordshire ;o))))) Nitey nite x

Urgh it's **3am!!** Jack's snoring must have woken me up. But, what an amazing dream I've just had!!!
I was in a boat - a little rowing boat in the bay. It was a sunny day and I was enjoying just bobbing about hearing the water slosh around underneath me when suddenly I had a visitor. I scrambled to the side and peeked over, and there was Nic Nic! She had come to say hello. I recognised her straight away by her fin

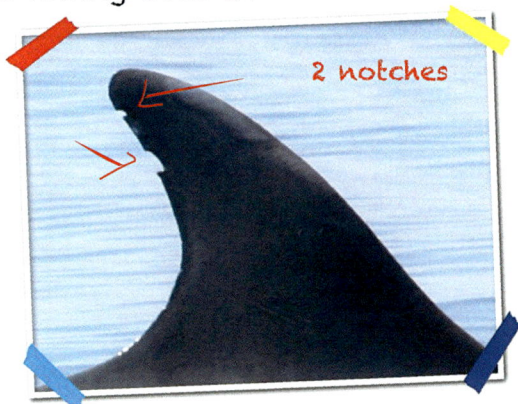

2 notches

which has two notches in it. It's why she's called 'Nic Nic'!

Anyway, she told me to follow her because she had something very important she wanted me to see, so I did. I rowed my little boat further and further out to sea keeping an eye on her ahead. I wasn't afraid at all because I knew she would keep me safe. We stopped and she told me to wait until she returned. She was very excited and it wasn't long before I saw her heading back towards me, but this time she wasn't alone. "*I've brought someone to meet you*", she explained, "*someone very special.*" It was the cutest little thing I have EVER seen. A new, very shiny, tiny little baby dolphin!!! Her baby!! It reminded me of a very young lamb when they have only just learned to walk. It was splashing about all over the place, knocking into its mum and disappearing under the surface then suddenly coming up again all smiley. I reached out to touch it. Nic Nic didn't seem to mind. I managed to stroke its little head and it squeaked and grinned back at me. She said I could name him. Well, I knew straight away what it should be called – Button, because it was the shiny button of Cardigan!! Nic Nic said it was an excellent name and Button seemed very pleased with it too. It was the best dream I have EVER had, EVER!!!!

3. An Interesting Encounter!

My mum watched over me every minute of every day. She taught me how to swim, making sure I used up as little energy as possible. When travelling along, she always made sure she swam slowly so we could stay within a fin's distance away from each other, with me always close by her pectoral fin.

"*If you stay right up close to me, right by my side then you'll get away with doing very little*" she chirped, encouragingly, whilst gently touching my side with her fin. I looked up at her, feeling confused.

"*What I mean is I am doing most of the hard work for you,*" she explained. "*As I'm much larger than you, I'm pushing most of the water out of our way so you can just be carried along in my 'slipstream'*" she grinned, "*Now, isn't that clever!*"

'*Slipstream...*' I thought about it for a moment, 'yes, I liked the sound of that!'

So we spent many hours swimming around practising the 'slipstream travelling' technique. I enjoyed it a great deal as it gave me a chance to look around at my surroundings.

Most of the time all I saw was more and more water, occasional rocks scattered here and there and sometimes random silky, green plants floated along in the water column. I snapped at those just within my reach as they passed by in the current. Sometimes I would let them go again and watch them float away but other times I carried them around in my beak as a token of my journey that day.

Sometimes I noticed that the water was not always dark and featureless but could sparkle. I was told it was the sun that shone down from the sky. Everything looked beautiful when it shone and suddenly I could see hundreds of tiny particles in the water. It painted a whole different picture of this watery world, it seemed to come alive. Dancing light on the rocks and stones, sunny beams reaching down through the water as we swam together, highlighting all the other tiny creatures that lived alongside me, and most of all, the warmth I felt on my skin as we surfaced to breathe was delightful.

Mum taught me what some of her 'clicks' and 'clacks' meant so that I too could begin to communicate back to her. I also discovered I could whistle…yeah really whistle! Mum called it 'my special whistle' that was unique to me so that she always knew exactly where I was. She whistled and then I had to whistle in return. She said we must practise this a great deal. So for the first few weeks we were both whistling to each other every single minute of every day until in the end I knew exactly what hers sounded like and she, mine.

Those first few days were tricky I won't deny it. Try as I might to steer successfully using my floppy fins, I ended up floundering and wavering about until sometimes I didn't know if I was upside down, sideways on, or inside out. I found myself criss-crossing in wild frantic movements in front of and over Mum's head in a desperate attempt to keep up. But Mum always came to my rescue, gently nudging me back in the right direction and keeping me on course by pressing her fin against my side.

"*There, there, my little one*" she whistled, as she patted me on my head with her fin. "*You'll tie yourself up in knots if you keep that up*" she chirped and chuckled.

With all these new skills to learn, I hadn't had much of an opportunity to investigate my local surroundings in greater detail. This watery world that we lived in was full of sights and hundreds and hundreds of sounds, many of which made me jump out of my skin. On closer inspection I found out that we shared the bay with lots of other creatures beside ourselves and those microscopic ones I had discovered in the sunlight.

Poking around in some rocks one day, minding my own business, I spotted something scuttle out and then stop dead in its tracks.

"*Yeahhh?*", it snarled at me angrily whilst waving two nasty looking snappers in my face. "*What are you staring at, eh?*" SNAP SNAP, SNAP SNAP.

I couldn't take my eyes off this strange looking creature and began to circle it so I could examine it from all angles. The more I looked, the angrier it became, and it started to shake itself frantically and wildly and snapped its claws faster and faster, and each time closer to my beak.

"*How funny you are!*" I couldn't help but burst out, "*You're such a tiny little spiny thing. What are you?*" I chuckled and clicked, "*and why are you so angry?*"

"*Funny....FUNNY!*" he furiously shrieked, red-faced, "*I'll give you funny.*"

And before I could do anything, I felt a sharp pain and let out the most piercing "*OOUUCHHHHIIEEE*" as this strange little critter had attached itself to the end of my beak and was squeezing very hard indeed. Quickly, without thinking, I rammed my beak deep into the sandy bottom and began to try to violently shake it off.

"*Let go, you spiteful snap-happy sneak!*" I clacked loudly between shakes. "*Get off, this minute*", but instead he gripped tighter, saying,

"*There, that'll teach you to laugh at me, that'll teach you to call me FUNNY and to go poking that UGLY, long beak of yours into the business of others!*" he squawked hysterically.

Although the grip that he had on me certainly hurt a great deal, it was also beginning to tickle because in his determination to stay attached, he shifted and fidgeted his pincers about. In fact it tickled so much that I began to laugh and laugh and laugh. I laughed so hard that I was blindly bumping into rocks and stones unable to see where I was going. This of course made the little creature more furious than ever, which made me laugh harder. My belly, my sides, and everything ached.

"Oh, please" I begged him, *"you just HAVE to let go, you're ti..., tick....,* *tickling me,"* I tried to explain through fits of hiccups and giggles, *"I can't* *take it for another minute more!"*

With all this going on, I had quite forgotten to surface for breath and was now gasping. Quickly deserting the ocean floor and making for the surface, still with this creature attached to my beak, I broke through for air.

"Ahhhhhhhh" I went as I sucked in a great belly full through my blow hole. I would NEVER forget to do that again!

"Oh no, Oh no, you fool!" screamed the critter in sheer terror quickly relaxing his grip and letting go of me. I followed him as he slowly floated back down towards the seabed.

"If they see me up there, they'll make crab meat outta me!" he wailed, as he descended, all eight legs now floating above him as he gained speed, and dropped like a stone.

"Who's they?" I snapped sharply, getting a little annoyed at being called 'a fool'. Whoever was a fool, I was certain I was not one of them. *"Don't* *you know?"* he stared at me in amazement once he'd arrived back on the ground more than a little shaken. *"Crabs like me become sandwiches if we* *are caught up there!"* he screeched, hopping from one claw to another.

And as quickly as he'd arrived, he scuttled back towards his rocks and disappeared, leaving a puff of fine white sand behind him. I looked upwards to where we had been. I wasn't sure who 'they' were or what sandwiches were either but I was sure it wasn't all as bad as the critter had made out.

4.   A Bit about the Bay & Three Firm Friends

We bottlenose dolphins stay in a relatively shallow, sandy-bottomed bay called Cardigan Bay, with stretches of sand in between rocks and gravel.

One sunny afternoon, Mum and I were out cruising when we bumped into aunt Grace, aunt Lilly, and a few of my cousins. I was getting used to dolphin greetings, some of which consisted of touching fins and rubbing ourselves together. It's how we say *'good to see you'* and *'how've you been?'* Dolphins are very tactile and love to gather in groups. They also can't be on the move all the while and need quality napping and resting time. So we stayed and hung out at the surface with one another. It was lovely feeling the sun's rays on my back. It was often at social times like this that I learned a great deal from my family group, including all about Cardigan Bay.

Apparently, we bottlenose dolphins have lived in the bay for hundreds of years. It's the large amounts of tasty fish that first attracted us here. In the summer months we love the taste of conger eel, mullet and salmon, mixed later with mackerel, and sea bass, but in the winter most of us move further north to find the rich shoals of whiting and spawning herring.

"The Cardigan Bay group is the largest group of bottlenose dolphins in these waters", boasted Cousin Holly. She had heard this from one of the many dolphins who visit us occasionally from outside of the bay - known as the 'offshore' dolphins.

*"The CB group (*Cardigan Bay group), *gets even bigger in the winter; sometimes there are over one hundred of us gathered together"* she continued, *"and around the coast of Wales can be as many as two or three hundred of us in total."*

'*Wowww*', I thought, feeling my eyes becoming larger. So I lived in a group of a few hundred individuals, and I only knew a handful of them so far! How exciting.

Sometimes when congregating in family groups, certain individuals would perform a strange ritual. 'Rock rubbing' consisted of swimming to the nearest cluster of large stones or rocks and vigorously rubbing themselves on it. It seemed to be a very pleasurable thing to do to the point where the individual doing the rubbing would almost forget to breathe. It would often take up a great deal of time because it seemed that once they had begun, the delight of it was so intense that they quite literally couldn't stop. Today was no exception.

"*Ooooooh that's lovely. Lovely, lovely, lovely*" grunted Cousin Swift after she had sidled up to a rough looking outcrop and was now totally involved in her rub.

"*There is nothing quite like a good rub, Button. You'll see when you get older. It is simply a miracle cure for any itches, niggles, bites or scratches*" she grunted again, as the water around her began to fill with flaky skin and it became more and more difficult to see her through it all.

"Teeeeeee-rribly good for the skin too" she continued, rubbing harder *"It sloughs off all the dead cells leaving it clean and algal clear. See?"* she clicked, holding up a fin for me to inspect.

So I was slowly learning how to be a dolphin. Also I was beginning to understand how a dolphin filled its day. Fishing seemed to be the most important activity, closely followed by travelling, hanging out, forming friendship groups and gathering news, scratching itches which might occur seven or more times a day, antagonising curious sea creatures and of course surfacing to breathe, which really should be at the top of my list because a dolphin cannot live if it cannot breathe.

However, this list is not yet complete, as I was about to find out about another important and truly wondrous dolphin activity…

I met many other dolphins during this time, two of them being just a little older than myself:

Tigger, whose mum is called Chris,

and Lumpy, whose mum is called Smoothy.

Sometimes they both joined me and my mum, whilst their mothers went off to find food. I occasionally had to join their little group whilst Mum went in search of food too. Although I bitterly complained about being left, she explained that without food she would become very weak and would not be able to make enough milk to feed me properly. And as I was such a hungry boy, this just would not do. So I would watch her from afar as she danced from one cluster of rocks to another, skilfully discovering fish and other strange looking creatures, and greedily gobbling them down.

I didn't like the look of this type of food, much preferring to nestle into my mother's stomach and guzzle down her rich milk.

"If you continue to drink like that, then you'll soon be bigger than your father" she chirped, but not really minding that I was always hungry.

It was a calm sunny day in late summer. I was growing up and spending a little less time at my mother's side although we were never far apart.

My newfound firm friends and I were just discovering another side to a dolphin's life…play time!

It was the newest addition to my 'dolphin activities' list and oh what an activity it was! We spent hours frolicking about. Our first game, we thought, was a winner... we called it tag and had immense fun tearing endlessly about, chasing each other around and around, and tagging each other with our beaks. I had to stop and rest because I was feeling quite dizzy after a long stint of being the 'tagger', and trying to 'tag' either one of them.

Next was a great game that Tigger had seen other dolphins playing whilst out with his mum one afternoon. He told us to stay right where we were whilst he swam off to fetch something.

Lumpy and I didn't have to wait long before Tigger returned, carrying a piece of thick, ropey, green seaweed tightly in his beak. He called it 'the tug tug game' and told Lumpy to take one end of the weed in his beak whilst he continued to hold the other end. I had to count to three, and then the two had to pull as hard as they could. The winner was simply the one who got the weed. Well it was the funniest thing I've ever seen. Lumpy pulled, then Tigger pulled harder, then Lumpy, re-adjusting his grip on the weed, seemed to gain control again. Then just as it looked like an even battle, 'Snap', the weed broke in two, and both my friends went tumbling backwards bumping beaks and tails as they went. What a game!

Lumpy was very confident, and quite a bit larger and rounder than me.

For this reason, Tigger and I nicknamed him 'Plumpy'!

Plumpy delighted in telling us what to do and how to do it. When the games didn't quite go his way, he would suddenly change all the rules and blast off with a great swipe of his tail to his mum, leaving us there clicking with laughter.

Tigger was quieter and smaller and when Plumpy disappeared off in a fury, Tigger and I just hung out, mimicking each other's actions and movements, and making up secret signals together. For example, one signal was a quick nod of the head which meant *'look behind you'*. Another was turning our bellies in towards each other, quickly flashing the white part. This meant that we were pleased to see each other.

Signals are one way we communicate to each other and are a very important language for a dolphin to learn. Another way is to talk. We make noises in our heads and then project them out so others can hear them. We make many, many different types of noises, from grunts and squeaks, clicks and clacks to chirps and whistles, but I only knew a handful of them at this stage.

However, I was about to learn a new one!

'Wwweeeeeee Hhhhheeeeeee' came the almighty piercing noise from below us as Tigger and I got the shock of our lives. Plumpy came rocketing past us in a lunatic fashion, totally out of control and making a mad dash for the surface. He was drumming his tail hard, up and down, up and down, and somehow managed to launch himself clean out of the water and then totally disappeared, only to come crashing back down a few seconds later with an almighty belly flop.

"WOW! That was awesome" he squeaked excitedly, belly turning pink. *"Did you see that?"*…unable to stay still in one spot due to the excitement of it all. Not waiting for an answer, he vanished back down to the sea floor only to launch himself out of the water for a second time.

We dashed to the surface to see how high he was jumping. He was totally clearing our heads and it looked like excellent fun.

'Ttthhhhhwhhhaackk' the water went as he collided with it on his way down, stomach first.

"Oh man, you gotta have a go!" stomach now glowing red. Tigger and I didn't need any more encouragement.

'Whiiiiiizzzzzzzzzzzzz',
I was flying! Actually flying through the air. I was completely out of the water and everything looked very different from so high up. I tried to look around me but it all disappeared in a flash as I came hurtling back down again.

'SPLATTT', went the water, as the first thing to hit it on the way down was my belly.

"Ouch, that was sore" I winced, turning to Tigger, but he was so busy, propelling himself up again, to hear me.

What a wonderful time, and with practice we got much better at launching, leaping and diving back in until there wasn't a single belly-flop in sight.

This new activity briefly took us out of our world. Out of the sea and into a different world altogether. It was a place I had visited many times for air so I named it the air-world, but so far I had kept my eyes shut. I'm not sure why I did this, maybe I was afraid. Anyway, entering it like this meant I was there for longer. More time to open my eyes, more time to look around. I wasn't sure about this place. I wasn't sure about it one little bit.

5.   A Dramatic First Day!

Sunday 20th June – First full day in Dolphin land!!! Yipeeee

9am and rudely awoken by a strange '*Tap, tap.........tap*' noise. At first I wasn't sure where I was.

'*Tap, tap.........tap........tap, tap, Crraaaaaaaaaa, craa, craa, craa, tap, tap.........tap........tap, tap, craaaa cra cra cra*', it went again and again.

I really laughed when it woke Jack up too. "*Damn birds!*" he mumbled, and chucked one of his pillows at the window where a really HUGE herring gull stood tapping on the glass. '*Oi, wake up, wake up*' I reckon it was squawking. When it didn't fly off, Jack got <u>really</u> huffy, and grunted "*Don't know about 'Dolphin View', more like 'damned annoying herring gull'.*" So I sneaked out of bed and crept towards the foot of his bed, then quickly ran my nail along the bottom of his foot! That REALLY wound him up ;o)))))

His mood became even worse when I skipped to the window and threw open the curtains. Jack groaned and told me to shut them immediately or he would launch me out of them. He's way too much of a chicken to actually do it though, so I flapped my arms and made chicken clucking noises around his head!!!

The view was even better than yesterday. New Quay looked half-asleep but the houses were very bright with the sun bouncing off their coloured walls. The sea was shimmering and sparkling. I wanted to use the binoculars but Dad had warned me that I should never look at the sun through them because I could blind myself, so I gave it a miss. I opened the window, and perched myself on the sill inside. It was heaven with the warm breeze on my face. I couldn't wait to go into the village to explore. I'd seen tons of photos of New Quay on the internet, and was desperate to get out there now, to run on the beach and swim in the sea.

Oh yeah... What about the strange dream from last night! Me, being out in that little boat, and wouldn't it be odd if Nic Nic really has had a baby!? Very weird. Better not tell Jack.

He'll say I'm a looney-tunes and should be locked-up.....better go, Dad's calling us for breakfast.

12pm Midday – At last they're done with breakfast, it only took 2 hours!!! What were they doing, growing the baked beans?!! But at last we're finally ready to set off and explore!! Yay ;o)

We started by checking out the town. I love the little coloured cottages all perched like little soldiers along the cliffs. I'd love to live in one, perhaps in pale blue, and I'd sit in the window and look out to sea all day long.

Each one is a different colour - pink like candyfloss, green just like mum's pea soup (YUKK :oP), yellows and sky-blues, not like the boring brick houses back home. The windows and front doors have white painted edges and each has a little front garden, with crooked wooden fences around them. I wish we could have the same plants and flowers growing in our garden but mum said that these were special coastal-dwelling plants that could only grow by the sea. She said she loved the smell of the honeysuckles and jasmines. I did too.

Jack kept moaning 'cos he wanted to visit the amusement arcade. What a LOSER!

This place is awesome! Everyone at school will be soooooo jealous when they see this diary, and I've only just begun. Oh, and I've started to take quite a lot of photos too with my HAPPY SNAPPY!!

Next stop, the beach...

36

...The sand is golden and the closer I got, it looked as if a fairy had gone around with a wand, tapping out sparkly white powder here and there. I took my sandals off and stepped onto it. It was warm and soooo soft. I sat on a dry patch and ran my hands through it. It felt all silky between my fingers.

At the edges of the beach there were rocks which grew into larger rocks, and I could see lots of children busy with nets on long sticks and buckets. Rock-pooling! COOLIO!! I have never been rock-pooling, but saw it on TV once. They found sooooo many creatures like crabs, tiny fish, snails and then there were these weird red, blobby, jelly things that squirted at you if you upset them. Oh, and also Crumpets (or was it limpets??) anyway the ones that live in a pointy shell, and stick like concrete to the rock when you try pull them off.

Amazing Fact   Limpets eat at night (think they munch on algae or something?) Anyway, once they've roamed around all over the place looking for food and have eaten enough, they return back to EXACTLY the same spot they left and stick themselves back down again. How on earth does a limpet (or a crumpet) know exactly where it lives, when rocks all look the same??

Then, as if things couldn't get any better, we went to the quay to find out about....wait for it...BOAT TRIPS!

It's the little blue boat that we'll be going out in. I've seen it in the newsletters ;o)

5pm – We are now sitting on a huge hill that runs straight down, over the edge of the cliff and into the sea. I went to the edge with dad. It was well scary!! I could hardly look down.

Jack called me a wimp and kept singing "Lucy is a wet wimp" over and over. GRRRRRR, I HATE BOYS!!!!

We plonked ourselves down with our paper cones stuffed with salt and vinegary-chips. I LOVE the little crispy-crunchy ones at the bottom of the bag. SCRUMMY. Even Jack seems to be enjoying himself...pinching my chips /o(

Luckily I remembered to bring the dolphin booklet with me. This is a miracle 'cos I forget EVERYTHING. I even forgot to take my pyjama bottoms off when I went to school once!!! I'm not thick. I just have lots of other things going on in my head, that's all. I can't help it if all I can think about is dolphins - pretty much all day long. Mum says I'm 'dolphin mad'. Anyway, back to the booklet...It said that the signs to look out for when dolphin spotting was the flash of a dark-coloured fin, or the splash of white water as the head breaks the surface. There was NO WAY I was going to miss the chance of spotting something.

Copied from the booklet ...
'The best conditions for cetacean spotting are flat calm seas. Any movement of a whale or dolphin is more easily visible when waves or white horses are not present.'

Why would there be horses out there? And why only white ones? Weird! Or is it just me being slow again??

Oh well, the conditions are just right'. The sea is flat, like a mirror. I can hear very gentle waves from the beach below. The only thing that doesn't seem right to me is the buzzing noise which is coming from the speedboats and jet skis. They are really loud. Sometimes I can hear the people on them screaming and shrieking, especially the girls. Soooooo immature.

It says....
'Boat traffic, like jet skis and speed boats, can keep dolphins away, as they can become disorientated by the high noise level, particularly if there are several boats moving erati-kally erratically at the same time. Dolphins have also been known to suffer injuries due to accidental vessel and propeller strikes, especially very sociable animals that often approach boats.

I asked Dad to take a photo of them for me, in case I need it for evidence! There was no way I was going near the edge of the cliff again!!

Here's more information I might need...

Sometimes, dolphins will breach, which is an awesome thing to see. They can leap right out of the water, landing with a splash.

The next thing was...

"*OH LUCY!!*" cried Mum, "Lucy did you see that?" "*YES, YES, I did, I DID*" I burst out, jumping to my feet in excitement, then everyone joined me. It was mad!! We were all jumping up and down, even Jack!!

I saw them next.. "*THERE! There it is again!*" I cried, pointing to where a dolphin jumped right out of the sea. Then suddenly another jumped, and a third, making large splashes on the surface. By this time I was so excited I felt out of control, thinking I might jump in with them!

For the next hour we all just sat there, like dummies staring out to sea. We totally forgot about our chips. Mum said it was the most wonderful wildlife spectacular (spectacle?) of our lives.

My first ever photo of dolphins!!!!! My heart was beating so fast I could hardly hold the camera steady. Dad says it's a brilliant photo, and I should enter it into a competition ;o)))))))))

6. Alien Craft

We had agreed to spend the day playing. Tigger and I were being 'dolphin sat' by Plumpy's mum, Smoothy, whilst Mum and Chris went off for food.

It started out as every normal play day, with Plumpy ordering Tigger and me about whilst we tried our best not to pin him to the seabed with our beaks.

There was something different though. I was finding it very hard to concentrate on our game 'signal the signal' because of all the noise coming from up above.

"What is that buzzing noise?" I whistled Tigger eventually, after deciding to take a break from the game to investigate.

Along with the buzzing came the dark shadows that whizzed over our heads one way, then the other. I hadn't noticed this before. Turning myself onto my side to get a clearer view of the surface and, sure enough, there it was again, *'ddrrrreeeeeeeezzzzzzzzzzzz'* as it flew along churning up the water above us.

Tigger joined me, also staring up, watching these strange objects criss-crossing our sky. I had come across many of the creatures that lived alongside us in the bay but this one was completely new to me.

"Do you think it's one of those dangerous predators that Plumpy was telling us about?" I whistled, suddenly feeling afraid.

"Yeahhhh, it could be stalking us" replied Tigger, looking worried, *"waiting until one of us goes up for air and then it'll make its move and POUNCE!"*

Just as I was signalling that it was perhaps time to find my mum, Plumpy's whistle rose up from far behind us.

"Well I think you two are sissies. Come on... it's an excellent chance for an adventure. It's called 'dodge', and I saw the older ones playing it just yesterday - looked like great fun."

I wasn't so sure and felt anxious that Tigger's mum would wonder where we'd disappeared to. After all, she was supposed to be on 'calf watch'.

"Sissy's, sissy's, sissy's..." Plumpy went on.

Tigger and I both knew what was coming next...

So up we all started to swim.

Popping our heads just above the surface of the water, we could make out many curious objects travelling about. Some were large and made a deep rumbling noise as they travelled slowly along; others moved much more quickly, nipping and zigzagging around, tearing up the water and making an awfully loud and high-pitched buzzing noise. These objects seemed to bounce off the surface of the water as they flew, and with each bounce came the sound of screaming and squealing.

The noise made by these curious things sounded quite different when heard above water. In fact when I tried to click to Plumpy, he didn't hear me at all, above or below the water.

Each object had one or two odd forms positioned on them which moved about, and many of them appeared to own two gangly attachments either side of them, which waved about frantically, the faster the object flew.

"*Aliens*" clicked Plumpy knowingly.

"*Cooooorrr*" replied Tigger, looking around in a trance-like state. "*They're aliens from the air world*", clicked Plumpy again, "*and those are their craft, that's how they get about.*" "*Wow,*" Tigger was transfixed. All three of us bobbed in the water staring around us for some time, "*OK, Plumpy, how do we play this 'dodge' game then?*" I quickly chirped hoping to bring us all round.

Well we didn't get the chance to learn the rules or discover the object of 'dodge', because the next thing was that I had caught sight of one of these alien craft out of the corner of my eye and it seemed to be heading straight for us.

Travelling at an alarming pace, it was very quickly closing the gap and gaining on us. It didn't look at all like a creature, as we had originally thought from down below. It was definitely an alien craft, with aliens aboard!

Quickly retreating to just below the surface, I could now clearly see a round spinning object viciously cutting through the water. Tigger was in a complete trance, staring with huge eyes as it approached.

"*Quick!*" I squealed, feeling that this was not a good place to be, and seeing the rotating blades coming closer and closer until they loomed right over us. I could almost feel the force of it on my back. In a blind panic we banged into each other and flailed around. Fins and tails at all angles, we managed to dive down as fast as we could, bubbles whizzing past my eyes, and the noise of the craft vibrating in my ears. After a few seconds of madly flapping my tail, I thought I must have made it. I stopped. I looked. I was ok! Oh the joy, I was ok. It was a near miss but we had made it.

"*Oh Plumpy!*" I chirped. "*Thank goodness...that was totally terrifying, but thank goodness we're ok.*"

"*Ahhhhhhhh*" came the piercing high-pitched whistling scream. Quickly turning around, I saw Tigger frantically trying to look around at his dorsal fin. As I looked, the water had started to turn a dark red colour. I was terrified as he seemed to be writhing around in pain and was sinking fast.

"*Ahhhhhhhhhhh, Ahhhhh*" the screams came again and my eyes followed the red trail he was leaving. Down, down and down it went.

Tigger hadn't dived quite fast enough.

"*Tigger*" I whistled, "*TIGGER!*" again. No reply. The water was so cloudy by now that I could barely see anything. Desperately wondering what I could do, I remembered the sonar communication technique that Mum had begun to teach me. Wildly I began clicking as hard and fast as I could in every direction:

"*Clickclickclickclickclickclickclick*".

My head felt like it was vibrating. Still nothing, as my clicks disappeared into the abyss. Panicking, I let out another round of sonar "*Clickclickclickclickclickclickclick*".

Suddenly from the depths, I felt a very faint returning click. Quickly, Lumpy and I tried to follow it but being very inexperienced with understanding the messages sent through sonar, I was unsure where his reply had come from or from how far away. A few more faint clicks were returned which we could just about make out and I was sure to click back in return to let Tigger know we had heard him and were coming.

Lumpy and I frantically searched the area that we thought Tigger had disappeared to. No more clicks. It was like searching in a muddy pool. We ran out of air so had to surface.

It was then that Lumpy's mum approached, looking very cross,

"I whistled, and whistled, Lumpy! Why did you not reply? I had no idea where you all had disappeared to. One minute you were right beside me, then the next...gone!" Lumpy looked down at the seabed, *"it was the noisy craft above"* he replied, very quietly. *"And what are you both doing now? How am I supposed to look after you all when you go sneaking off like that..hmmm? Talking about all, where is Tigger?"* she snapped.

We had to find Tigger … I just hoped we weren't too late…

7. A Shocking Event!

8pm – Can't believe what happened today! I'm still in shock, everyone is.

The dolphins were happy and free one minute, then the next...It was awful, I can't stop thinking about it.

I remember I was watching them closely through the binoculars. Mum said I was giving excellent commentary...

"*One, two, three.. yes there are still three of them*" I counted out loud. "*What are they doing now?*" Jack asked. "*There's a boat*" I heard myself say, "*It seems to be heading ...... heading straight for the dolphins!*"

Sure enough we could all see a speedboat and it was travelling as fast as a rocket, straight for the little group. It didn't seem to be aware of the dolphins at all, and the dolphins looked like they hadn't seen the boat either.

I grabbed my snappy and took loads of photos. Here's the best one.

Mum began screeching "*Oh my God, we've got to do something*". She tried jumping up and down waving her arms above her head and shouting "*STOP*". I joined in, "*Stop, watch the dolphins!*" But it was no good. We must have looked like tiny ants on that huge hill.

Dad thought they might be ok as they are wild animals and must have some knowledge of these dangers, but the boat kept coming and they didn't move!!

I don't know how, but I managed to keep the binoculars just about steady enough to see what was going on, tho all I really wanted to do was cover my eyes. One dolphin definitely managed to get away because I saw its head and tail dive under the water in front of the boat. I think the second one also managed to escape by leaping to the side, but only just. But I was sure the third hadn't been so lucky. I was positive I saw the boat hit it.

Mum said that we must tell somebody. She was sure there would be someone who could help to perhaps find the animal and save it. She was right, 'cos back on the quay we saw a girl with binoculars and a cool 'I am a Dolphin Defender' T-shirt, and we told her the story. She wrote it all down and said it was brilliant that we'd managed to take photos of the whole thing. I told her that I had adopted Nic Nic and hoped it wasn't her or her baby who'd been hit! I'm not sure why I said this! Think it just slipped out, but she just stared at me. Then she asked how I'd known that Nic Nic had had a baby. I felt my face getting hot and knew it was glowing bright red. She must have thought I was a right weirdo. All I could do was stare at the ground. Felt like a complete numbskull! She asked again and said it was very strange because the dolphin researchers had only just discovered she'd given birth, and hadn't mentioned it to the public yet. By then everyone was staring at me. I mumbled something about it being just a guess. She laughed and said it was an amazing guess as the dolphins usually only have calves once every three years or even longer. She was still looking at me funny when she told us to expect a phone call because she was sure the dolphin would be ok, and she would get a boat out to the exact location ~~imediatly~~ immediately.

On the way home everyone was very quiet and I felt like they were wondering what I'd been up to. My head was spinning. Thank goodness Jack broke the silence by telling us all a story he'd read on the internet about how a whale had once been hit by a massive ship, and had survived even though everyone had said it wouldn't. It's so dangerous for them out there!! Especially when they are babies and the sea is full of idiots who think they rule! The girl from the quay said there are always a lot more boats around during the summer holidays and a lot of the people in them have never even been on a boat before let alone driven one!! I'd NEVER do that. Jack said he wouldn't either.

10pm - I'm really tired and going to bed in a mo'. But just before I sign off...I know my eyes looked red earlier 'cos they still do, and they feel all puffy too so maybe Jan, from our B&B had noticed. She heard us coming in and wanted to know what had happened, so we told her everything.

She seemed to know a lot about the dolphins and told us all about how they communicate. They can talk to each other over really long distances. Owen is her husband and is a fisherman. Apparently he sometimes hears them when he's out on his boat in the dead calm, whistling and calling to one another. He says it's like being surrounded by magic.

Then her face went all sad. She told us that there are loads of dangers out there for them. She said some even drown!!! I didn't know dolphins could drown! I thought they were brilliant swimmers. Some of the babies die because they are starving, and others just disappear. Owen told her that he's seen babies without their mums, and once he found one washed up on the beach, dead. It was so young it still had the stripes around its body where it had been folded up safe inside its mum's tum, so together they named it Stripey. I felt like I could cry when she told us that and she had tears in her eyes too.

I thought it was strange that she said the waters around Wales were safe though. I don't really understand how they can be safe if dolphins die in them!!

Mum told her about Nic Nic's baby and how I had known about it before anyone else. She bent down in front of me and looked me straight in the eyes and said Cardigan Bay is full of magic. Everywhere the dolphins go, they bring magic and they have special powers too. Then she leaned over very close to my ear and whispered, "They choose very special people to show their magic to Lucy, not everyone sees it." She winked at me and told me to keep my eyes open for the magic.

8.   The Search is on!

The 'missing dolphins' alert went up in the bay and before long a large group of dolphins had congregated around us.

Chris was really distressed, swimming up and down whistling to herself,

"Poor, poor Tigger! Please don't let it happen again! Just please don't let it happen again!"

I overheard Mum telling Smoothy that Chris had lost her first baby, Stripey, three years ago. It was only a few weeks old, and had somehow gone missing. The CB gang searched for weeks but no trace of her was ever found. Chris had spent along time afterwards all alone scouring the areas she had last been with him, not understanding that he was dead but only that he was missing.

Six months later, she became pregnant again and Tigger was born. But after hearing this I was scared. What if Tigger was never to return, like Stripey! What if it was all my fault. I could have warned him earlier to dive. I should have searched harder for him.

Nervously, I quickly went over the story and told how Tigger was now lost and possibly dead; the surrounding group listened gravely. Some clicked comments in reply, others remained silent.

This was a serious problem, of that I was certain. Plumpy and I looked down at the sea-bed. We felt ashamed.

Finally, an elder of the group piped up from the back,

"We understand a great deal about these alien-craft strikes now to know that they are not always fatal. It is the tail of the craft that is of most danger to us, the limb that 'propels' it along" he explained seriously. *"Although one has to be mindful of the entire craft, one blow from the front end can render a dolphin unconscious, and we all know what that means"* he whistled gravely, and certain members of the group whistled in agreement. The elder continued, *"As one gets older, one learns to avoid the front ends as well as those sharp propellers which can cause devastating and wicked blows to a dolphin's fin, flukes or back. However, all is not lost for Tigger. We must organise a search and it must commence with urgency."*

So, 'Operation Search Tigger' was well underway within no time. Many dolphins were now involved, departing in groups of different sizes. A wide area of the bay was to be covered, the older and more experienced would go offshore whilst the younger dolphins remained with their mums closely following the coastline.

Lumpy went with mum Smoothy, Coral searched with her mum Topnotch, and I stayed very close to mum whilst my older brother Splash went off with his little friendship group making up a strong male trio.

It was like no relaxed little jaunt that I had ever known. Mum moved quickly and fluidly through the water like I have never seen her do before, frequently changing direction and expertly weaving in and out of rocks and large clumps of seaweed, all the time whistling and echolocating in burst pulses of clicks, and investigating *everything* with her beak. I had a job to keep up! I used all my strength, beat my tail as hard as I could, and twisted and turned my flippers to quickly manoeuvre myself. I even did the odd leap and jump to help keep up.

The silver sides of fish flashed as they fled in terror, thinking they had narrowly escaped our jaws, but it was not food we were searching for this time. Because of the speed at which we were travelling, we had to continuously surface for air. I knew Tigger's life depended on all of us and there was a strange sense of uncertainty in the water. I was determined that we should save my playmate no matter what.

It was very dark now and the sea was choppy and hard work, but on we travelled. Mum, pressing ahead, concentrating and serious. We had found nothing, no trace of Tigger and no clues either. All seemed quiet as we scouted around some large rocks, when suddenly I heard a most peculiar noise from very close by,

'*Aaaarrrrrgghhh Aaarrrgghh Aaarrrgghh*' it went.

I lifted my head further out of the water to try to get a glimpse of where this strange noise was coming from or from what.

Next I heard a scratching and scraping, and then again - '*Aaaarrrrrgghhh Aaarrrgghh Aaarrrgghh*'. Mum was busy checking a sea-weedy spot nearby, which I was quite pleased about as I desperately needed a rest. So whilst carefully avoiding being pushed into the rocks in the rising swell, I came closer to them, keeping my head low in the water in case I had to make a quick exit. The noises continued, and adding to them was one which sounded like a sort of slapping or flapping....'*fluuuu 'ump, fluuuu 'ump*'.

We rested for a while, although I found it very difficult to sleep due to the continuous racket that was being made right through the night, *'fluuuu 'ump, fluuuu 'ump'* it went.

Morning came, I remembered where we were and what we were doing. The noisy rocks were now noisier and as I looked more closely, I could see some movement. The flickering of....a fin! A fin similar to mine was waving about. Then....a tail! Also similar to mine it was now dangling over the edge of one rock and was flapping about.

"Tigger!" I whistled, *"Tigger! Quick, Mum, I've found Tigger!"* I had no idea that dolphins could venture onto rocks! How had Tigger got up there? Maybe the waves had forced him there or maybe he had been pushed? *"Oh Tigger, thank goodness you're alive!"*

'Aaaarrrrrgghhh Aaarrrgghh flump flump flop flop flop ....SPLASHhhh'

'Hang on a minute? Tigger looked strange, I thought. Darker than I remembered and, well, just not quite right somehow.' I now doubted whether this was Tigger at all, but whatever it was, it was with me in the water and swirling around eyeing me up!

"It's nothing to worry about, Button" clicked Mum in amusement, watching me staring in bewilderment at the creature who had joined me in the sea.

The creature, was clearly not Tigger, to my great disappointment. Its eyes

were larger than mine and it seemed to have many thick white hairs sprouting from its face.

Before I knew it, it had swum swiftly underneath me and had launched itself back up onto the rocks above and continued with its strange wailing noises. It was swift, I'll give it that. I could now see there were many of them up there, all lying lazily about on what looked to me to be a very sharp and uncomfortable platform, but they seemed more than happy with their choice of resting place and blended in very well with the black rocks.

Mum told me that they were the grey seals of the bay and were of no harm to me. She spoke with them. They had heard a dolphin pass by them many hours ago, whistling, but added that it had been dark and the wind had howled through the craggy rocks and so they were unsure whether it had been a trick of the wind.

Weary, disappointed and needing food, Mum began to lead the long way back to our patch. She despondently snatched at small fish on the way to keep her energy up.

The others had all had a very similar experience to us - a long, cold night with no success. Splash thought he'd seen a young dolphin but then realised it was a porpoise. Smoothy thought she'd seen him with a group of dolphins but then realised it was only some friendly common dolphin visitors, and Topnotch was almost certain she had seen Tigger behind some rocks but then out swam a large group of seals who had been searching for fish. It was a very disappointing time but we were all determined to keep searching.

That night I dreamt of Tigger. There he lay, in a hunched up pile somewhere on the seabed. The water around him was dyed red, and the pain in his fin sharp and stabbing. He looked around, weak and frightened.

It was the first time he had *ever* been on his own. In my dream, the sea looked dark and menacing without his mum or friends nearby. Feeling the need to breathe, he tried lifting himself up a little bit at a time off the sand, and very gently rocked his fins back and forth until he started to rise. He knew that to move his tail would have been far too painful. Once at the surface, he inhaled a large but gentle breath.

Looking around he could see he had been pulled along in the strengthening current and no longer recognised his surroundings. 'How far have I gone?' he asked himself, looking about in despair.

The dream continued...It became darker. The sun had all but disappeared apart from some faint pink smudges across the sky. Everything was quiet.

His fin hurt him terribly and he was tiring through shock and lack of food. He could barely keep his eyes open.

Dolphins are very clever creatures. One dolphin fact that not many people know is that we are able to sleep whilst remaining awake! How can that be? Well a dolphin has a wonderful and curious brain that consists of two separate sides. One side sleeps while the other stays awake - a very useful thing when one lives in water!

"Thank goodness' he clicked to himself with a large sigh through his blowhole. All was quiet."

So Tigger let the waves rock him from side to side as day turned to night. The last few oystercatchers flew overhead piping to each other as they went. He gazed up at the darkening sky and at the stars that were beginning to appear. Some were clustered closely together forming shapes and twinkling brightly but others were alone in the huge black sky, dim and hopeless. Tigger sighed, he could do nothing but allow the sleep he so badly needed, to take over.

9. Out at Sea

Monday 22nd June, 10am – We're in the breakfast room. It's really noisy. I think there are some new guests who are excited about their holiday. They're all laughing and joking.

None of us feel like laughing! I can't swallow my food. Everything's sticking in my throat, and the smells are making me feel sick. For once Mum and Dad aren't bothered that I'm not eating because they don't look too hungry themselves.

Uh, that made me jump....the phone's ringing. Mum's scrabbling about in her hand bag... She's always scrabbling about in that bag!! She calls it her 'bottomless-pit' and usually misses all her calls by the time she's found the phone!!

Hee hee, Jack's rolling his eyes at me. I can't help but snigger. I LOVE that word S N I G G E R.

Everyone's looking at mum. *"Well?"* asked Dad, as she hung up. No news yet...blast!!

11.30am – WOWZERS!!! We're going out... on a boat!!! Jack and I are waiting for Mum and Dad who are still getting ready upstairs. It all happened really fast. We were the last ones still sat in the breakfast room (surprise, surprise), when a big man walked in. He smelt <u>REALLY</u> badly of fish.

He said we mustn't waste any more time and must get out there. I didn't have a clue who he was, or what he was talking about. To be honest I thought he was a bit strange and could hardly understand what he was saying with his strong Welsh accent. I couldn't help but burst into giggles, which started Jack off too!! But, then Jan walked in and said, *"I see you've met Owen, my husband"*. Ahhhh now it all made sense! Then she began handing out sets of bright yellow, rubbery outfits! Jack and I looked at each other and I knew he was thinking 'NO WAY! I won't be seen dead wearing this!' Then we exploded into more fits of giggles. Jan said it was nice to see us smiling and laughing again. It was nice to *be* smiling and laughing again!

So Owen had been told about the dolphin incident and decided that we should be 'pro-active'. He called us *his* 'Dolphin Defenders', and told us to grab some warm clothes and binoculars and meet him at the quay in twenty minutes. And that was that. I like being pro-active!! - Lucy, a defender of dolphins. ☺☺☺

I'm so excited. I can hardly believe we're going out in a proper boat, not just a little blow-up like the other kids on the beach. A REAL fisherman's boat!! Jack is also really chuffed. He loves boats, planes, helicopters and all that stuff. He's always going on about cars and engines so will probably bore everyone stupid, but I don't care, 'cos I'm going out to 'see the sea'!!

Jan's given me some HUGE packs of cheese and home-made chutney sandwiches to look after. She says it's important we eat because it could be a long day and once the sun disappears it'll get very cold. Jack's already eyeing them up...typical boy, all he can think about is his stomach!

Jan and Owen are so different to anyone I know back home. They are so friendly, and fun!! Here I feel that anything could happen...anything at all!!

12.30 - The quay was really busy with holiday makers. We finally saw Owen waving at us from a large, wooden boat and as we came closer I could read 'Golygfa Dolffin 2' on the side, in bright, swirly curly letters.

- Quick update... Owen knows EVERYONE! The fishermen, and people on boats all wave and shout over to him. I don't understand a word of it, it sounds like gobble-de-gook to me. Dad said it was the Welsh language. I had no idea Welsh people had a different language!

Anyway we are out of the harbour now and heading along the coast. The wind is stronger and the sea is choppier here and it's very hard to write! We're all smiling though ;o)))
Here we are on the boat, it's ACE! Owen reckons the sea state looks good for today. Not sure what that means but I nodded anyway, hee hee. I think he's trying to wind Mum up a bit cos he told her there's a brisk wind coming down from the north, and that it might get a bit interesting later on. Then he winked at Jack and I. Mum's face was a picture.

Ah, that's better...Owen's turned the engine off so we can all hear again. He's pointing out all the sea-birds to us. He's amazing, he knows every one of them just by the sound they make. I love their calls. There are kittiwakes, guillemots and razorbills. Check out my snappy of them on the cliffs. It's quite hard to see them because we couldn't get any closer.

Blimmin' heck, I've NEVER EVER seen anyone eat so fast!! I couldn't help staring. He saw me and laughed. He said there's no point wasting time when it comes to Jan's famous door-step sarnies, then pulled out another one and polished that off too! Even Jack looks impressed.

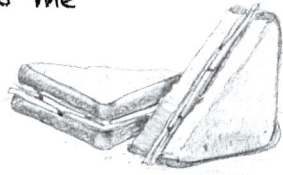

Between mouthfuls he's telling us all about the chat he had with the scientist gang this morning. I think he said that three calves were born very recently, but it's even harder to understand him now with a gob full of cheese! Hee hee

Note - three calves! Could it be the same ones that were involved in the boat crash? This is turning out to be a real mystery. Hey, this diary might end up being part of an invest-i-gation (investigation?? Oh whatever)!

So exciting!!!! Nothing EVER happens to me. Just hope that little calf is ok!

Owen explained to us that it's always great news when a calf is born. It means the dolphins are happy in the area. Happy enough to have babies. He also said these waters are fairly safe and have fewer threats than other areas. It's because other places have more people. Here in Wales there are fewer injuries, less pollution, and less over fishing (this is when humans catch more fish than we should and don't leave enough for the dolphins). So greedy!! He also said he's seen lots of near collisions by young kids showing off on jet skis and speed boats. I think they're mad. They don't think about the danger they are causing to the dolphins. Oh and to their STUPID selves!!!

Hang on a minute...who's that? I can hear someone's voice.....

Jack's just told us that Owen's got a call on his VHF radio. It's the scientist gang... they're saying that a large group of bottlenose dolphins has just been reported by a local fisherman. It's a really big group who look like they're on a mission. Owen's determined to find them! - He means business!!!!!!!! Wicked!

Off we go. I'm at the very front, ready for action!! I LOVE the feeling of the cold water splashing my skin, all salty when I lick my lips.

It feels like I am flying across a perfect surface like glass. The water is so clear, I can even see rocks and sand and sometimes sea weed. Faster, faster, faster & keeping eyes peeled!!

1.20pm - OMG. There are dolphins!!!! We found them, so AMAZING!!!!!!!!!!!!!!!!!!!. Catch you later.........

A long time later...
10.15pm I'm back at the B&B. What a day and I'm not tired at all! OK, so here's what happened...

So, I was standing at the front, just like Kate Winslet in Titanic!! It felt incredible. When all of a sudden... well I thought it was Jack at first playing a joke on me. A squirt of water all over my face but Jack wasn't anywhere near. There it was again but this time I saw where it was coming from!!! Then OWEN shouted,

"Dolphins!" and was pointing excitedly to the bow (the front of the boat if you don't know).

Everyone made a dash to where I was standing. We were all looking right, then left, then right again. It was mad.

My first EVER close up snap of a dolphin.
So gorgeous and happy xxx

XoXoXoXo

"Starboard!" Owen cried, but of course no one had a clue what that meant. So he pointed to the right side and then suddenly the most amazing thing happened. Out of the water jumped a beautiful bottlenose dolphin, right beside us!!!

I've never seen anything like it. It was HUGE and TOTALLY GORGEOUS. And it was smiling. I've even got a photo of it (and a squirt of water to prove it!)

Mum was nearly crying "It's incredible!" she kept saying in a high squeaky voice. Jack and I could hardly keep still, looking from left to right and saying things like, "There's one here." "And here!" "There's FOUR NOW!" "That one jumped right out."

Owen carried on travelling quite fast because he said they were enjoying the speed of the boat and bow riding. It was so amazing to watch them. They just seemed to move along with hardly any effort at all, and were even faster than we were! Some jumped and splashed and seemed to be loving every minute of it. He said that there were rules that all boat people had to follow when dolphins are around, but we were ok because they wanted to follow us and not the other way around!!

Another happy snappy. They were so close to the boat! We were surrounded!!

He counted at least 30 which he said was one of the largest groups he had ever seen. I have no clue how he knows that because I tried counting them but whenever I reached 5 I wasn't sure if I had counted some already or not and had to start again! It's very hard trying to count something that moves so fast, and also keeps disappearing!

Owen thought they might have stayed with us for longer though, like they normally do. He said it was odd because they seemed in a rush to get away even though they were enjoying themselves. I wonder why?

It was so awesome! What an experience, and guess what...there were 2 babies in the group!!!! Wooohoooo!

Hmmmm, actually the more I think about that!!

NOTE - why 2 and not 3???

It became quite windy after the dolphins left us. The sea was choppy and dark. We couldn't believe we'd been out for five hours already. Dolphin spotting makes you lose all track of

time! Owen said it was time to turn back. He wanted to head back along the coast to see if there was anything amiss. Well it didn't take long to find something...

Owen pointed to some huge rocks that stuck out of the sea. He said it was a well-known danger spot called 'the Cauldron', and many boats have come a cropper here (think this means they've crashed!!) People don't see the rocks that lie just below the surface – something to do with low and high tides??

I was sort of listening to what he was saying but there was something in the distance that I couldn't get my eyes off, and this next bit that I'm about to write is what really freaks me out.

"Look!" I said, pointing past the cauldron. Jack looked through the binoculars. There was a little white boat. A rowing boat. Owen said it was strange for such a small boat to be out here, on its own with no sign of an owner. He decided we should go for a closer look. I didn't need to go any closer. I already knew this boat. It was the very same little white boat from my dream. The one I had sat in! The one I had met Nic Nic and Button in! We drifted closer, and could see it was completely empty and was becoming damaged because it had been swept on to some rocks, which

stuck out of the sea by the entrance of a big, dark-looking cave. There was no one about. We shouted but there was no answer. Owen called the coast guard, saying he'd found a boat drifting around with no owner. They asked for a boat ID number but none of us could see anything at all, so they told us to tow it back to harbour and said it had probably come loose from a nearby bay and had drifted along in the current.

Owen came up close to it and asked Jack and I to help by tying a rope around the metal ring on the front, so that we could tow it back to shore. Jack managed to lean forward and grab the ring to try to steady it while I looped the rope around it. It wasn't easy because both boats were going up and down in the sea and it took me a couple of go's to get my timing right! As I turned to throw the rope back to Jack, something caught my eye. It was like a tiny little light that flashed brightly across my eyes. So, while Jack and co. were busy with the rope I turned back to the boat. There it was again. I looked harder and saw that there was something lying on the seat inside the boat, and when it rocked in the water the sun bounced off it making it glint. I checked no one was looking and leant forward as far as I could to try to reach it. My finger-tips nearly touched but not quite. Just a little bit further...and YES, got it! I stuffed my hand

66

quickly into my pocket and shivered. I knew at that moment that something very very strange was going on, and I somehow seemed to be a part of it.

I think it was about 9pm by the time we arrived back to harbour. We were all tired but still helped Owen dock the Golygfa Dolffin 2 (and its extra passenger – the boat!) We all thanked him for a wonderful day, and for helping us try to find the dolphin.

So now I'm sitting on my bed and I already know what's in my pocket. I don't even have to look to check. I can feel the arched shape of its back, the fin, and the strong tail that divides into two points at the end. I run my fingers over the stone design and as I take it out of my pocket the shiny pink, blue, green and purple stones twinkle and catch the light from my bedside lamp. It's so beautiful.

What with all the excitement and upset from the terrible event yesterday, I hadn't noticed that my dolphin pendant that hangs around my neck, was missing! It had been a present from Mum and Dad, and I'd worn it <u>every single day</u> for the past 5 months without fail, only ever taking it off for school swim on Mondays.

My hands are shaking as I turn it over. Hang on, this wasn't here before!! I can't stop reading the mysterious writing on the back. I'm sure I haven't made a mistake, it says –

'Dolphin Defender Lucy. Love Stripey XXX'.

Where on earth had this message come from and how had MY PENDANT ended up inside a boat that I'd never really been in, out at sea?!

I flip it back on to its front again. I can't take my eyes off the stones as I hold it up to the light between the tips of my fingers. The colours are amazing and seemed to be getting brighter as I watch, like the whole thing is glowing! I have NEVER seen it do this before!!

Wow, hang on...Is that water I can hear? It's like water rushing past me as if I am under it. And my eyes. I had to shut them quickly because keeping them open made me giddy. Yes, it was water, everywhere! Bubbles too, loads of them streaming past me. Then there was a whirring sound. It got louder so I knew it was coming closer. An ugly dark shape began spinning up ahead. It wouldn't be long before it reached me. Quick! I had to get out of the way!! But hang on. I'm not in danger. I'm only watching it all. I'm fine, apart from the burning feeling in my hand that is. I quickly looked down, the pendant is really glowing now! I could clearly see coloured light glinting out from between my fingers. I kept a strong hold of it. The tighter I held, the brighter it glowed and the warmer it became. I shut my eyes again. Images began flashing in front of them. The whirring noise is a spinning blade and is so close now, when suddenly it connected with something. Something real, warm and alive...and now sinking down and down into the black below. Red was all I could see. Dark red puffs like clouds rose up beside me. The whirring faded away and then came the strangest noises of all. Click, click, click, followed by lots of clicks and whistles. They were so high I had to hold my hands over my ears and my whole body vibrated! It was like being 'buzzed'! And I'm not quite sure, but, I think I may have also heard my name.

Then I saw it all. It was clear as a picture, like watching a film...

...I know exactly what happened to that little dolphin calf.

10.   What the Pendant told

Tigger was far out to sea, lost and with no land in sight.

Gently, he began to make his way down to the seabed. It was much further away compared to the light sandy-bottomed bay where he lived. It

was very, very dark and cold too. He shivered and looked around. All was black and deathly quiet. The bottom was rocky so he used his sonar to check the area out but found nothing helpful. *Kick and glide*, *kick and glide,* he went as he travelled back up to the lighter and brighter levels until his beak broke through into the air.

A little way off, he noticed some large birds - gannets his mum had told him, who seemed to be circling above a spot on the surface. As he swam nearer, he could see their big white wings dipped in black at the ends, soaring above and calling loudly to each other. '*Maybe it was a dolphin?*' he hoped, swimming a little faster. Maybe it was his friends! He knew that gannets often followed dolphins because, wherever dolphins were, there was usually food nearby and gannets were opportunists.

But to his huge disappointment, he found no familiar fins or tails, no beaks or heads. What he did see, though, was a mass of seaweed and fish, all seemed to be mixed together. The gannets squawked their warnings from above. '*Take off*' they called, '*Take off, it's ours.*'

Tigger dipped just below the surface and carefully turned himself onto his back and looked upwards. From this position he had a clear view of this interesting cluster above, and he tried his best to identify it better. There were definitely fish within the

matted ball, but they were rotting and falling apart. Only used to taking milk from his mum, he stared at the fish hungrily. Maybe he could try eating some to regain some energy, he wondered. His sonar revealed that the mass was somehow joined together, but by what he had no idea. He echolocated from the centre of the pile outwards, to try to find out more and he quickly discovered that the echoes that bounced back from the middle were strong, telling him it was a fairly solid thing. But, the further out he detected, the fainter the echoes became. It was very strange. There was definitely something in the water which seemed to stretch out a long distance but was totally invisible. He used his beak to nudge at it to see if that would give him any clues.

He could feel something. It was as if the water contained some sort of mesh. Curiously nudging further in, something seemed to be enveloping him and touching his skin. He lifted his head and felt it hanging from the end of his beak. Suddenly sensing that all was not right, he began to back out, but to his surprise, instead of being able to move away from it, he could see the rotting fish and seaweed following him. Shocked, he wriggled around trying to free himself. The fish and seaweed just came closer and were now wrapping themselves around his fin. Turning around and around hoping to shake it off his body, his tail then became entangled too. In a blind panic he forgot about the pain in his fin and started to bolt through the water, splashing and thrashing, whistling and shrieking.

The gannets were alarmed at the sight of their dinner being whisked away, and attempted to save it by diving, full force, at the moving heap. Tigger was frantic, and swam quickly down to try and get away from their sharp, stabbing beaks but still they came at him. Diving into the water at incredible speed, their wings held tightly by their sides, and eyes covered by a thin film of skin. They darted at and around him like missiles. Every time he tried to head in a different direction, they just stopped him in his tracks.

Deeper he dived, dragging the mass down with him into the deep where the gannets couldn't go.

'*Why were they attacking him*? He wondered desperately.

Very, very frightened, he cowered by a rock for safety, shaking and cold. '*What was this stuff that was attached to him and why did it keep following him around?*' Knowing he would have to return to the surface soon, he tried to pick out small pieces of seaweed and fish with his beak, tossing them aside, but they just floated down, wedging theselves back into the invisible web.

He swam along the bottom for a while, hoping it was far enough so that when he surfaced once more, the gannets would be gone, but with this extra load behind, it was hard work!

Relieved and thankful to discover that most of the birds had given up and moved on, he felt calmer. He was tired, hungry, cold, and scared though and barely able to move properly because of the stabbing pains in his dorsal fin. He soon realised that the more he wriggled to try to break free, the sharper the cuts into his fins, tail and beak became. He had no choice but to let the tide take him where it wanted whilst more and more seaweed collected behind him, weighing down his exhausted little body even more.

And so began another miserable, cold night with only the stars to tell him he was still alive.

I sat in our bedroom, the pendant still warm in my shaking hand. It had shown me everything. I'd watched the whole thing unfold in front of my eyes. I had reached out to try to help him but I wasn't really there so could do nothing!

I understood *everything* I'd seen. It was like a jigsaw that needed to be pieced together with the earlier parts from when we had all sat on the hill watching three little calves playing in the bay. Through the binoculars I had seen the calf disappear under the boat. So, he *had* been hit as I had thought! It was the spinning blades of the boat propeller that had caught him. Then to make the situation even worse, a discarded fishing net allowed to float along in the water had wrapped itself around his body, trapping him like a wild animal in a cage.

The last few stones have stopped glowing now. I'm so tired. Must sleep.

11. Teamwork

'Operation Search Tigger' was already well underway for the second night running. The group had gone off in their various directions. Mum and I took off in the opposite direction to the previous night, but again hugged the coastline.

We hadn't been out very long when...

"Button, you must try to keep up" whistled Mum,*"time is running out."*

I was trying my best! We had already scoured a large section of rocky coastline but I was hungry! Mum stopped to let me suckle. Dad had said I was growing and developing nicely, building up good amounts of blubber 'to help keep me warm' and muscle to give me that famous 'dolphin athleticism' that he was so well known for. I was also becoming better at preserving my energy by using the new 'kick and glide' swimming technique which was still a bit of a novelty for me.

Suddenly, a ghostly whistling travelled across the water. I stopped drinking. Mum became very still. It came again. We moved towards the sound.

"*Stop*" hissed Mum, "*I can feel something.*" So we stopped and waited. I couldn't *feel* anything. "*There, there it is again*" and with that Mum was off, the seabed flashing past below us. We surfaced. We listened.

'*Oooooooooooo*', came the ghostly whistling again, clear as day this time, '*ooooooooooooooooooooo*' across the water. We were near some huge rocks which towered above us and I could see a large dark opening straight ahead.

"*Button, stay there*" squeaked Mum, insisting that I don't move a fin or a tail, and away she went towards the rocks. The last I saw was her dorsal fin disappearing into the black hole and then she was gone. Not for long I hoped! My eyes didn't budge from that spot.

It was a while later before she returned,

"*We have no time to lose, Button. You must follow me as quickly as you can. Tigger is in REAL danger. Remember… NO TIME TO LOSE!*"

So, we travelled like no dolphin's business, following the coast back to the bay.

Tuesday 23rd June, 11pm – Me again...it's our fourth night in New Quay and what with the surreal dreams, mysterious boats, secret messages, and magical mind-blowing pendants, I haven't slept a wink. Not surprising really! The weirdness going on around here is enough to freak anyone out. I don't know what's real, dream or magic anymore!!

The latest crazy thing to happen was when Jack came running across the beach towards me today in a right state. His eyes were huge, and he was puffing and panting. He'd been fishing along the coastal path when all of a sudden he heard a ghostly wailing type of noise. He said it seemed to just float across the water towards him, really freaked him out. Now Jack is not one to go telling stories, and would HATE to look like a wimp so it did surprise me.

He said it went on and on to the point where he was sure someone was playing a joke on him, or even that it might have been some local kids trying to scare him off their fishing patch. With the noise becoming louder he tried to play it cool, slowly packed up his stuff and wandered away pretending he was looking for a better spot, but it was when he heard the calling; 'Luuuuuccccyy come' that he fled, 'as fast as he bleedin' well could' were his exact words, not caring what he looked like. When he told me, I just remember my mouth dropping open, the bucket falling from my hand with a 'fluuupp' sound as it hit the wet sand below. Everything seemed to slow down, right down like slo-mo. He had said 'Luuuuucccyy' in exactly the same way that I had heard it last night through the pendant. I haven't been able to stop touching my magic pendant all day since last night. What is going on around here and why is this happening to me??

Mum said I didn't look well at all, had gone a ghastly white colour and sent me indoors for a lie-down. I think I'm going mad! Nothing would surprise me anymore, not even a talking dolphin.

Jack's awake! I can just about make out his silhouette in the moonlight. Think it might be time to fill him in on a thing or two!!

11.30pm We decided that the thought of not doing anything to investigate this mystery was too much to bear, especially as we'd had no news from anyone about the calf. I'd been shown the whole truth of what had happened to it and felt that if we left it much longer it might be too late. So what was stopping us?? Well, we'd probably get in to a pile of trouble for sneaking around at night (but that was nothing new!) There was also the teeny tiny matter of borrowing just a few small tools from Owen's boat that might come in very useful (rope, torch, boat hook, etc etc)! But, I'm sure this will be ok...gulp.

So after talking through our options the decision to go is final. We're going to return to Jack's fishing spot to see if we can see or hear anything. I'm pretty sure I know where this is anyway and that it's the same place we'll find the little fella...if he's still alive that is. So, if we make it back within a few hours, no one will even know that we've been out....so nothing lost. On the other hand, if there *is* something there, we could return in daylight with man-power (one of Jack's sayings... typical!!) Anyway, a good decision!!

Well, we're ready. It's midnight. The cobbled streets are cold and wet - warm clothes on and lots of layers! This will be my last note for a few hours (actually, I'll take my diary

just in case I'm stuck somewhere with nothing to do, or nobody to talk to! And DEFINITELY taking the magic pendant!!! It's <u>very</u> safely tucked in to my pocket.

12.30pm We've stopped so I've got a few minutes to keep you all up to date..

Jack and I made it to the quay. It was damp and cold and I was having serious second thoughts! All I could think about was my lovely, snuggly warm bed, until...

Jack spotted two dolphins very close by - in fact they were right by the quay wall. One was absolutely tiny ;o) No bigger than me. I had a feeling I knew who this was. Jack heard them first.."*Listen Lucce...they're whistling, can you hear?*" he said.

I wasted no time in pointing the torchlight at the larger dolphin. It stayed still enough for me to see quite clearly who it was. Yup, I was right. I'd recognise that fin anywhere. My beautiful Nic Nic ;o)) She had come.. I knew she would! We both understood each other. She whistled, flicked her head - it was simple, we were to follow.

As we approached the coast where the aliens leave their craft, we heard some strange sounds coming from one of them. Hang on...there was a head! What sort of animal was that I wondered? Not a seal, nor a dolphin, nor a crab or a porpoise…then another head.

"*Stay close Button*" Mum chirped, "*they are the alien type, the ones from the air world…these ones are nice though.*"

Mum began swimming on her side past these alien creatures to get a closer look. As she did this, the two beings also came closer. Mum

spouted some sea water at them. This had the most curious effect upon them; their faces sort of creased up and with that came a peculiar sound. A little bit like our chirping when we are pleased to see one another. Then the smaller one reached out to us. I recognised this as being a similar gesture to the one that *we* make when greeting others, touching fins. Mum began to whistle. I joined in. Again the faces creased up, the chirping, gurgling noise was made, and they reached out further to us– I thought this was a good sign.

I copied Mum and spouted water at them. We then swam and they moved quickly along beside us. We turned and swam back, and they followed! I was enjoying this game very much!

Mum manoeuvred herself in the water so she pointed up towards the moon and started to whistle loudly. She clicked also, and then began flicking her head in the direction that we had just come from. What was she doing? The alien beings looked at her but stayed still. Mum repeated this strange dance but this time swam off in the direction that she was nodding. I joined in but wasn't sure of the purpose of this new game or why we were spending so much time playing it when we had been in such a hurry earlier to try to save Tigger, but it was fun nevertheless. Suddenly, they began to follow us. Mum whistled louder. They whistled back, following quicker and quicker behind us. Mum continued to click, whistle and head flick, so did I.

Loaded with tools and other bits from Owen's boat, we moved quickly along the coastal footpath. Sometimes it led high up onto the cliffs, but then it would drop down again into a bay or cove. Streams tinkled and sparkled in the moonlight as they ran down from the hills to join the sea. I didn't take my eyes off the dolphins as we walked.

Like I said, I already knew what our mission was that evening. I think Jack was beginning to cotton on too... "*Do you think they might know where the other one is?*" he asked. I knew that dolphins were one of the most intelligent animals on the planet. "*Why not?*" I replied "*if you knew that one of your friends was in trouble, wouldn't you try to tell someone?*"

It was a serious trudge I can tell you. Up hills, over streams, around rocks. We'd already been out for an hour and all this time the dolphins had remained close by, continuously whistling across the sea whilst we whistled in return, but then the whistles stopped, the dolphins had stopped.

We stood staring out to sea unsure of what to do next, when suddenly,

'BOOM'

"*Listen!*" I hissed, suddenly standing bolt upright with my finger up to my lips... the noise made the hairs on the back of my neck stand right up.
Then about thirty seconds later,

'BOOM'

"*What on earth...?*" Jack cocked his head to one side,

'BOOM'

"*Hang on.....look at the waves. Every time a wave comes in to shore...*"

'BOOM'

"*It's a cave Luce!*" he exclaimed excitedly. Yup, he was right. It was *the* cave. The one that we'd seen from Owen's boat yesterday! So, was this yet another sign (a clue perhaps)...my pendant ending up in that little rowing boat right outside this cave? But why here? Jack couldn't believe he'd walked that far earlier with all his fishing tackle and hadn't realised he'd been standing right above it, all that time. Doh!!

The booming noise was made by the waves entering the cave and hitting the rocks at the back. It made me shiver. But why had the dolphins stopped here?

Mum demanded that I wait outside the cave whilst she go in to see if Tigger was still there.

I couldn't see the alien beings any more but that was because I was tucked in amongst some rocks for safety.

Mum returned. "*He's there, but he's in a very bad way*" she clicked, "*we don't have long at all now before he will die.*"

12. A Heavy Load

Wednesday 24ᵗʰ June, 1.15am

I wish I could have gone down first, after all it was because of me that we were here, but Jack wouldn't have it so I had to agree. I knew it was *probably* the best plan anyway even though I hated admitting it. Jack's bigger and stronger, and he'd also done some rock climbing in the past so it made sense. The plan was that he'd go down to the cave opening and see what was about.

He chose the longest rope we had, put a loop at one end to go around his waist and tied the other end to a large rock and pulled very hard. He leaned right back onto the heels of his feet, letting the rope take his weight. I have to say I was impressed, it was strong. I could see he was really pleased with himself – boy's stuff ;o)) There was no way I'd have known how to make a safety harness. Every knot I'd ever tied came loose as soon as someone pulled it. He took the brightest torch and told me to stay where I was, and to keep an eye on him with the remaining torch. He would holla' up if he needed help, and with that he began to carefully descend down the jagged rock face, which led to the cave below.

So here I am, waiting at the top of the cliff in the blackness. Now that we are actually out here doing it, I have to tell you I am scared. It's a very real fear. Not like a fear when you watch a horror film, or the moment before you plummet down from the top of a roller-coaster, but this is a 'what if' fear. I can see the whites of the waves just below him and the splashes making their way higher and higher up the cliff. He seemed to be doing well though, until he began to make his way around to the entrance of the cave. That was where I lost sight of him, hidden by some large, overhanging rocks.

Still can't see him. I keep shouting his name and moving the torch beam across the edges of rock, but still no reply. A horrible feeling's spreading over me. Jack hasn't told me what I should do if something does happen. I have no idea! Up here, alone not knowing what's going on...thank goodness I brought my diary, otherwise I reckon I'll go maaa...

Oh thank goodness for that!!! I can see the top of his head again.

Jack thinks he's seen something in the cave!

Something moving around...

A few seconds later...he says the dolphins have returned! Apparently they're whistling and swimming in and out of the cave. I'm sooooo jealous. Why couldn't it have been me down there instead of being stuck up here and not able to see any of the action, "Well, just hurry up, it's getting late", I shouted bossily back.

Not only is it very late but the weather is changing too. It's not calm anymore. The wind is whistling along the tops of the cliffs and large drops of rain are beginning to fall from the black sky, some right down the back of my neck! Yuk!

I've just spotted something out to sea, a churning and boiling of the water. Of course, it's the Cauldron! I gave a shudder imagining what it would be like to be someone on a ship who hadn't known it was there.

HATE being up here on my own, my imagination's going bonkers!

Yay! One of the aliens from the air world is coming down to see us! Mum had cleverly led them all the way to the cave, all the way to Tigger. So it hadn't been a new dance or a game we had been playing earlier. There had actually been a point to all our efforts.

I was allowed to go into the cave with Mum this time and was very shocked at what I saw. Poor Tigger. How on earth had this happened? What a state he was in. I couldn't see too much of him due to the tangled mess he seemed to be floating in. I'm not even sure he saw or recognised me.

"We need to keep him at the surface, it's very important that we help him breathe" whistled Mum, as she swam underneath the floating mass of seaweed and rotting fish to help lift him higher up in the water. She couldn't stay there for too long though, as she was battling the increasing swell in the cave and needed air herself. I too was having difficulties to avoid being swept to the back of the cave where Mum said *I MUST NOT GO*, or even worse, into the web that held Tigger so tightly. I wasn't sure what to do! Mum continued trying to lift him to the surface but I could see it was very hard work as he was so heavy, being weighed down by all of the rubbish, and she had to be very careful that she didn't get caught up in it all too.

"Be brave now, Button and, swim out and find the alien beings. It's time. We need their help now. We cannot do this on our own. If we don't get Tigger out of here quickly and free from this...this trap, he will die for sure. Go now, Button, don't be long, and be sure to return straight back to me" whistled Mum.

I could see Mum was feeling very nervous about me going off alone, but she knew that this was the only way. With all the swimming we had done whilst searching for Tigger, I had become quite competent and made good progress through the incoming swell and out of the entrance of the cave.

"No, don't go!" I clicked as loudly as possible to the alien being who was now ascending back up the rock face. *"No...not yet, please, we need your help, please come back!"* I whistled over the crashing of the waves on the rocks.

3am - EVERYTHING's gone wrong. I'm terrified, freezing, and afraid for our lives.

Just as I had been trying to lower the boat hook down from the top of the cliff for him to grab...

"JACK!" I screeched. I had seen the whole thing unfold in front of my eyes.

Jack had turned around, I presume to see where the whistling was coming from and as he did so, he must have misplaced his foot. Suddenly he was slipping. Slipping down out of control towards the rocks and swelling sea. Stones and shingle slid from beneath his feet and bounced noisily down the rock face, plopping into the swirling water below. I even watched as he tried to grab at the rocks as he went by but they were sharp and useless. He fell through the air, heading towards the blackness below.

"JAAAAAAAAAAAAAAACCCCKKK!" I screamed.

All I could hear was the whistling of the dolphin. What should I do? My mind was racing. It would take me an age to get back to town and return with help, by which time Jack would surely be drowned. That was if he was in the water. He could well be dashed upon the rocks, bleeding, unconscious or even dead!

There was nothing for it, I had no choice. "I can do it" I said to myself, "I must do it", and with that, I grabbed a second rope from the pile and with shaking hands tried my best to tie a knot, as Jack had done, and slipped the loop over my head and shoulders, lowering it to where it sat around my waist. Tying the other end off from the same rock that Jack had used, I placed the torch into my back pocket, and stuck the boat hook into the back of my jeans.

I began my wobbly descent.

I hadn't received any replies to my screams, I tried to hurry. The rocks that I clung to were sharp and hurt my hands, and the salt spray was stinging my eyes. I was seriously beginning to regret my decision and, with a surging dread growing inside me, stopped suddenly, totally gripped by fear.

Shaking with fright, I tried to turn my head so I could look down but this made it worse. The sea swirled and beckoned to me, as if it was trying to draw me in to it. I truly believed I was going to fall, but going for help was also out of the question because I was stuck, not able to go up or down.

"JACK" I screamed, as I forced myself to look down again, just as his limp body bobbed up in the water below.

It must have been the sight Jack's body bobbing around in the sea that spurred me on. Nothing else would have made me peel my fingers off that awful rock face and continue down. With skill and strength that I didn't know I had, I slid easily down, using the same technique that Jack used in his rock climbing classes, and before I knew it, I was standing safely at the bottom. With no time to think, I looked out to where he'd been floating but he was nowhere to be seen. A sickening panic rose deep within me as I realised I could well be too late. Rushing to the edge of the water, and about to throw myself in, when all of a sudden a fin appeared within an arm's reach away and a 'phhooooosshhh' of water spouted into the air. Button the tiny little calf was there! I didn't think twice, I just threw myself towards it and made a grab for its fin. Sure enough he allowed me to hold on, and off we went. I could hardly believe that this was happening and was starting to wonder if I was totally dreaming it all (nightmare more like)!

Away from the cave, away from the shore. I was being battered by waves from all directions and quickly learned to keep my mouth tightly shut. Suddenly I saw what I thought was a body lifted high on a wave. The image of The Cauldron filled my mind, with Jack dashed upon it. That was where the current was taking him! It wasn't far, and Button seemed to know exactly where to go. Within seconds we were alongside him. Holding on as tightly as I possibly could to Button's fin, I reached out and my fingers grabbed for Jack's body. I clutched his clothing and with an enormous effort I pulled him towards us. Luckily he was face up but didn't seem to be breathing. There was no way I could pull his body on to the dolphin, I just had to hold on to him and try to keep him facing up. I'm not sure how little Button managed to swim so well under our weight, or how it knew exactly what to do but we were now heading quickly back to shore.

I slid off his back, and tried to support Jack's body but it was too much. He weighed a ton so I had no choice but to leave him while I dragged myself on to the shore. But as I turned back around expecting to see Jack sinking again, there was the little calf, supporting Jack's head and shoulders. All that was left was for me to get him out of the water – not an easy task!
Dream or not, it all seemed very real to me.

Somehow I knew instantly what to do with the alien body that was sinking to the bottom of the sea. Copying what Mum was doing with Tigger, I swam underneath it and began to lift it up to the surface.

'*Oh dear, Oh dear*', it weighed a ton weight and was jolly hard work to keep balanced. It seemed to be heavier at one end which meant it kept rolling off my back. I was worried as Mum would be wondering where I was, and I was pretty sure that this hadn't been her plan! Wasn't this alien supposed to be helping us? But, instead, it seemed to be in terrible danger itself.

The other alien was on the shore, good job as well because I wasn't sure how long I could keep this up! Out stretched a gangly limb, and the ends began to wiggle towards me. I swam with the being on my back towards the shore but the body began to sink again. There was nothing for it, I scooped it up with my beak and began to lift it once more. Exhausted now, I tried one more time to move it towards the alien being who was waiting - this time with success! The shore-based alien had managed to get a grip of my heavy load and was dragging it off my back. I could see this was very difficult so I tried to help by nudging it with my beak. It was a relief to be rid of the dead weight and I felt that at last the being was safe. Now I had to quickly go and tell mum the bad news – that the aliens had troubles of their own!

I was frantic, hysterical, although I managed to keep dragging his body up the beach until finally he flopped over. Jack's blank face stared up at me and it nearly made me scream. I'd never seen a person like this before, especially not my own brother.

It was the tiny flicker in his eyes that brought me back. I pinched his nose and breathed one large breath into his mouth. His chest swelled. I tried again, and again and again and then somehow, don't ask me how, he was coughing up water. I couldn't believe my eyes.

I grabbed him. I had been SOOOO terrified that he was dead. All I could think was how was I going to tell Mum and Dad, all his friends, all our family. The thought had made me feel sick to my stomach and everywhere else.

Sometime later between coughs and splutters, he asked me what had happened, so I turned to show him who had saved his life, but the little calf had gone. I was so disappointed. I stood up to look for it. It was then I saw the blood.

The whole area around Jack's lower body was filling up with blood! Everything went out of focus. I felt sick, so quickly sat down. I'd never seen so much blood and tried to trace it to find out where it was coming from. There was a tear in his trousers. Poking out of what looked like a very large open gash in his leg was a white, splintered looking thing. It was difficult to see what was what but I could see enough to tell me he had badly broken his leg.

So we are stuck at the bottom of the rock-face. I have all the time in the world to write my story because escape is impossible. I knew the tide turned every six hours. Back at the harbour at midnight it had been a low tide which was why I was now standing in ankle-deep seawater at 3.30am! I had no idea what to do. So far, I had instinctively known to roll Jack's body over, to give mouth-to-mouth, and thank goodness that had worked. I had also taken two of my layers off. One to cover and keep him warm and the other had been tied very tightly around his leg, over the wound to try to stop the bleeding. But now I was lost. I had to get help. That was the only answer - but how? I looked back up at the way we had come down. There was no way Jack was going to be able to climb back up the rocks. I wasn't even sure that I would manage it, and even if I had managed to climb the cliff face and make it back into town, Jack's body would probably be washed away by the time help came. Is it time to give up? It's only now that I realise how important this diary has been to me. I hope it will keep me going, and if it doesn't...well at least others can read about what happened to us and how amazing the dolphins were.

I held on tightly to my pendant, willing Stripey to help us.

13. A Tricky Operation

"Where have you been Button? I told you not to be long!" clicked Mum, in *very* short, snappy clicks. In a panic I explained what had happened with the alien being and she listened quietly, and then with her fin she touched my side, briefly. It helped to calm me down.

"Now, what we need to do is to carefully push Tigger out of here and towards the alien beings. If they see him, they might help. It's an alien trap that he is caught in after all, so they should know how to get it off him."

With Mum swimming underneath, supporting him, and me remaining close alongside to guide them, we began to move Tigger. I knew he was scared and hurting because of the sad, soft wailing noises that he made, and from the blood that ran from him into the sea. I tried to comfort him by softly whistling all the while. For one brief moment his sad, half-open eye looked at me. I wondered what he was thinking. I whistled louder and touched the end of his beak with mine.

We managed to get him out of the cave with few problems, and now it was my job to whistle to the alien beings again to get their attention whilst Mum continued to support Tigger. They saw us immediately, pointing their gangly limbs in our direction. The smaller one came over towards us. I swam straight up to it and those wiggly digits reached over and touched my beak, then further up to my head, very gentle. They were now stroking my side and fin. I quite forgot what I was there for, until Mum chirped out,

"Button, we are running out of time, I cannot hold Tigger much longer. I can't feel him breathing any more either."

Quickly, I flicked my head towards Tigger, whistling in long, high pitched tones to try to make this being understand that we also needed help. Suddenly the wiggly digits lifted to its face, covering most of it. The being then turned to the other. Did they not understand? I must whistle louder…I must get my message across somehow. I took the end of the debris that enveloped Tigger's body and tugged at it, to try to show them.... this seemed to have a good effect. The smaller one reached out to us. But there was a further problem. It couldn't reach. We moved Tigger closer to shore. It reached out again, this time waving some sort of long stick. That did the trick. Now Tigger was close enough for them to touch.

"He's barely breathing now, Button. I'm not holding out much hope for him, I'm afraid" clicked Mum, with a look I'd never seen on her face before. Her fin reached out and touched mine and she let out the saddest noise I'd ever heard.

I didn't have long to feel sorry for myself..

"Jack, quickly! I've got to do something to try to help it. Please tell me what to do!" I cried in desperation, and hardly able to see through floods of tears. Jack nodded to his back pocket, said he had a pen knife. I could see where this was going!

Rolling him over to get to the knife was a nightmare. I can't imagine how painful it must have been, but he didn't scream. There was more blood though. I was nearly sick.

He showed me how to open the knife and how to use it without injuring myself and, looking into my eyes, said;

"It's up to you now, Luce. You can do it. Don't worry about me. I can wait. This whole peculiar week has been all about this one moment. Now's your chance! I'll help you from here....quickly now."

I began to try to untangle the mess that surrounded the little creature. I had to remove the huge amounts of seaweed before I could even see the netting that had wrapped itself around it. It was a very slow process, and its little eyes were remaining closed for longer and longer periods. He was losing all strength. I knew I must hurry.

It seemed to be taking forever. My fingers were stiff from cold, and my arms were smeared in filthy rotting fish and slime but Jack egged me on from where he was.

With all the seaweed gone, I could see some of the damage that the netting had inflicted on its body. There was no way of pulling the net off its bloodied and injured flippers because it had cut through the skin so deeply in parts that I was afraid of causing more pain.

So I started to cut through the lines, using a sawing action away from the dolphin's body, taking care not to cause more damage. Nic Nic and Button stayed close by, watching and whistling. I understood that they trusted me and, like Jack, were also encouraging me. Briefly looking at the two calves, I could see just how young they both looked. Button, had pale bands around its little body, and as it opened its mouth to communicate, its little face smiled at me. How curious – where the corners of its mouth turned upwards just a fraction, there, in the crease of its skin, appeared a sort of dimple. A dolphin with a dimple, how cute! As I looked closer, it looked at me, opened its mouth wider and clicked gently. I had no idea what it was saying but the sound of the waves became louder, they were coming nearer. It had taken me an hour to free just one flipper. I had to hurry!

The sea was flooding in. Jack had water all around him. He was pale and dark under his eyes and his lips were turning blue. He said he was ok but I think he was trying to sound calmer than he actually felt. We would soon be in danger of being seriously caught out. Why can't the night come to an end? Shouldn't the tide turn in the other direction by now?

I continued with shaking hands. Poor little thing! The netting was completely transparent and wafer thin, no wonder the animal had got caught in it, I thought sadly. How on earth had it become loose in the sea? It must have been discarded and just been floating about. "It's a death trap to animals", I muttered, as a tear rolled down my cheek and I traced my finger delicately along a deep cut across its beak. How could someone have done this! I managed to free the dorsal fin, careful not to touch the deep wound that must have come from the boat incident. Then with the help of the boat hook I was able to flip the netting over and off the animal's body. This seemed to have an immediate effect on the dolphin because for the first time it slowly opened its eyes, just a tiny bit. I stroked its head, whispering to it as I worked. The other little dolphin whistled softly by my side.

I felt weak with hunger but knew I was going to have to get back into the sea to remove the last piece of netting which was wrapped around the dolphin's tail and flukes. I shook violently, and helplessly watched on as the last little patch of dry rocky shore became covered in sea water.

"We're going to drown, Jack" I whispered, whilst my shoulders shook with silent sobs...This time Jack said nothing.

The alien being climbed into the sea with me, Mum, and Tigger. I could see it was shaking. I nudged it to try to help it. It seemed very frail. Suddenly, it did something which was a complete surprise to me. I think it was swimming, or trying to as its limbs began to thrash about. It was now submerged and trying to pull at the net which held Tigger's tail tight. I was really pleased to see Tigger move his flippers, but also sad to see how cut and damaged they were.

"*Do you think he will be ok?*" I clicked to Mum, who was still looking deeply troubled. "*I don't know, Button, he is very……..WEAK!*"
Suddenly Mum was off again. This time she swam around to Tigger's face and nudged his beak with hers. There was no response. She nudged again, and this time he opened an eye. Mum rolled onto her side. Now I could see what she was trying to do! The problem was Tigger was so weak he could hardly move his head. I swam to him and nudged his beak and squeaked, "*Come on Tigger, come on Tiiiggger, you can do it…Plumpy would!*"

And then
to our
amazement,
he lifted his
head just enough
and began to suckle.

"HOORRAY!" I squeaked with glee, and did a little twirl and a leap for good measure.

Then, suddenly, I could see Tigger's tail was free too. In fact this alien being had now removed all of the netting from Tigger's body. I did a double leap with joy and swam over to the alien being and let it stroke my back while I nudged its limb. I clicked and clicked and clicked, I was so happy. These aliens obviously weren't all bad.

Tigger continued to drink. He drank and drank and drank, guzzling down Mum's rich milk. It made me feel hungry! He didn't even need support any more.

My job is done. I'm standing up to my knees in sea water, and Jack is almost totally submerged apart from his head and shoulders.

What I'd give for just a bite, just a tiny nibble of my sandwich that I scoffed when I was sat at the top of the cliff! What an idiot! I tried to climb the cliff earlier but had to give up. It was way too steep and slippery, and Jack had told me to stop as it was far too dangerous. All we could do now was sit and wait. For what though, I wasn't sure. A miracle, I supposed. I've collapsed next to Jack for body heat, not that he's got much!

Nic Nic is nowhere to be seen, but the two calves are very close by. The wounded one seems stronger after its enormous feed, and looks as if it has managed to come through the worst of its ordeal.

Button was gently stroking his friend with his fin. How amazing dolphins really are, one trying to calm and look after another. Sitting here with nothing to do, I started thinking. I thought of the curious goings on, and how real it all seemed. Where was all this magic coming from? Could it be possible that Stripey, the poor little dead calf, was now looking over us all - watching over the other dolphins and trying to keep them safe. I'm even wondering if he is a magic dolphin? Trying to stop what had happened to him, happening to any of the others. The more I thought about it, the more I reckoned it could definitely be possible and that the dolphin pendant was like a sort of object that he could communicate to me through. Maybe I had been chosen, like Jan had said, to be the one to help.

I want to talk to Jack, tell him my thoughts but he's too weak for all this. I will tell him when we are back at the Golygfa Dolfinn - when we are warm and dry. When we are safe again. Maybe it's the hunger getting to me now. I'm cold too, freezing actually. Maybe it has started affecting my brain (wot brain!) Right now, couldn't anything be possible? Was I even sitting here waiting to be rescued, or was this all a dream too? Had we really ventured out into the night and come all this way to this cave? Had I really just clambered down an almost vertical and crumbling rock face to save my drowning brother?

5.15am - Must have both dozed off! I opened one eye then the other, thought I was dreaming when I felt the glow of the sun on my face. Boy did my spirits rise as it fully appeared over the horizon. I shivered and tried to imagine feeling its full heat on me now, warming my freezing cold body.

"Lucy! Look the tide! Lucy, the tide is turning!" Jack cried, with as much excitement as he could manage without hurting his leg.

I stood up. Jack was right. The tide was finally turning and at last in our favour!!! The sea level has dropped about two

100

inches from its highest mark, and the sky is a brill clear deep blue.

Something else...Nic Nic is back! She has returned! She's joined the two calves again and is continuing to feed the wounded one.

Haaaang on.. what's that noise? I found the energy to drag myself onto some higher rocks to look out.

It was a sight I thought I'd never ever see again. I had prayed for a miracle, and, here, right in front of us, appeared one.

14. Reunited!

We're over here" I had shouted over and over, waving my arms madly. From around the corner came a wooden hull with the sun glinting off the side, highlighting the swirly, curly dots and dashes that spelled out:

'Golygfa Dolffin 2'.

But hang on. It wasn't going to stop! It hadn't seen us and was travelling straight past, "Over here, don't go, please!", I shouted as loudly as I possibly could. I had to do something to stop it, but what?? The sun shining in my eyes suddenly gave me an idea! Shoving my hand into the pocket of my jeans I searched for my pendant: where is it, where is it, I know I .....ahh got it. I held it between my thumb and forefinger.. Work, please work...! Dolphin magic, Stripey magic, work now, I muttered under my breath as I angled it towards the sun. Well, you'll never guess what...the boat only started to turn and headed right for us! The pendant was glowing! Stripey was listening!

"Mayday, Mayday, Mayday. This is Golygfa Dolffin Two, This is Golygfa Dolffin Two. Mayday" came Owen's voice over the VHF radio. "We have a medical emergency and require immediate assistance. Over."

No one said a lot whilst we all waited on the rocky shore, which was now much less waterlogged. But, there was a lot of crying. Mum and Dad hugged and held onto us tightly, and we stayed like that until the coastguard arrived.

It was a wonderfully fast and impressive speedboat with orange letters that glowed 'LIFE BOAT' down the side.

Three men jumped into a rib (Jack said that's what it was called), zoomed across to our rocky shore and stepped out to join us. They had been prepared for a medical emergency and, after taking one look at Jack, understood why.

The one that looked like 'the main man', 'the one in charge' wasn't happy! He was really scary!

"There was someone, or should I say *something* looking out for you today", he said. "A miracle I'd say" said another as he looked over at Nic Nic and then began to give gas and air to Jack to ease his pain whilst they carefully moved him onto a stretcher. "You have NO IDEA how lucky you both are!"

Dad went with Jack in the lifeboat, then the scary man smiled at me, probably because I looked terrified and he felt sorry for me. Think he knew we were in shock and had probably learned enough of a lesson to last us a lifetime.

I managed to explain, through sobs so heavy I could hardly breathe, that I'd prefer to travel back with Mum and Owen. I had a feeling the dolphins would follow the Golygfa Dolffin back to New Quay, and I wanted to be there, to watch over them, especially the injured one. So Owen assured me he would travel slowly so they could follow if they pleased.

On the trip back to New Quay I found out how we had been discovered and saved. Apparently Nic Nic had arrived in New Quay that morning and had headed straight for the Golygfa Dolffin 2 in the harbour. Owen had been getting ready for an early morning fishing trip when he saw her. He said she wouldn't leave the boat and that it was clear as day that the dolphin was trying to tell him something. She was clicking madly and making all manner of strange sounds that he'd NEVER heard a dolphin make before.

"She butted the side of my boat with her beak, she did" he laughed, "I've never seen anything like it!"

Then he looked at me really stern, I knew what he was about to say and I can't say I blame him. I suddenly felt ashamed and very silly. How could we have thought that going out on our own to save a dolphin was the right thing to do? To roam around in the dark in a place we didn't know, climbing down dangerous cliffs, and risking our lives! Not only that, but also putting poor Owen's life in danger by taking his tools.

He said it was unforgiveable to take a boating man's tools from his boat without asking or telling him. He knew he hadn't taken them because as every good skipper knows, you should always look after your tools and always put them back where they belong, otherwise in an emergency you'd be in one right, royal mess.

Mum piped in her bit – "just imagine if something had gone wrong for Owen out there on his own", nodding in the direction far out to sea, "and with no tools on board either!"

Anyway, it turns out that taking the tools had also been a good thing because it was when Owen noticed them gone that he realised there was something strange going on.

Everyone was worried sick about us when they found our room empty. So, straight back down to the harbour they went, jumping aboard the Golygfa Dolffin 2 where Nic Nic had waited patiently. Finding us was easy, they just let Nic Nic guide them.

"It wasn't all bad though," he said. "If it wasn't for the bravery of you, Lucy, and your brother, that little dolphin over there.." nodding towards the injured calf, "... would definitely not be here now, and that's another thing I know for sure."

The rest of the trip was in silence. I watched the three dolphins following in the wake behind us. I can't really explain how I felt. Sad that all this had happened, happy that we were all ok, confused because I didn't feel like the same old Lucy anymore, and blimmin hungry!!

Back in New Quay, word seemed to have got around about our adventure and the saving of not just one, but three, lives. Crowds were gathering on the quay, waiting for us to return. I was amazed to see so many people and suddenly felt very shy. Owen had warned us to expect a huge welcome back, and to expect to be treated like a celebrity for the remainder of the holiday. We could barely get out of the boat for flashing cameras, microphones being pointed in our faces, and TV people firing all sorts of questions at us. Jack gave a little interview from his stretcher for the TV cameras. He would be on TV screens around the whole world!! Then he was whisked away with Dad in the back of an ambulance to the hospital. Meanwhile I became totally surrounded by the crowd.

"It isn't us you should be calling heroes" I told them all bravely. "It's them out there" I turned and pointed out to sea, and to my amazement both Nic Nic and Button were leaping right out of the water... the press went wild snapping madly at them. "The dolphins...they are the true heroes of Cardigan Bay..." and everyone cheered!!!

We followed that alien craft all the way back to our spot in the bay, and, boy, was I pleased to be back. Tigger managed to keep up with occasional encouragement from Mum. There were many other aliens there when we arrived, not in their crafts on the water but all gathered together on land, so we didn't hang around for long. Anyway, Mum said she was famished. I was just pleased that Tigger was well and back home again.

Somehow the CB gang had all heard that Tigger had been found and saved, and had been gathering together. It was all very exciting and there was a great deal of clicking and clacking, and buzzing and chirping going on. There must have been well over fifty of us, including Dad, Aunty Lilly, Aunt Grace, older brother Splash and loads of others I hadn't yet met, and of course Tigger's mum.

She rushed past Mum and I, and Tigger immediately perked up. She checked him over very carefully with her sonar, paying more attention to the areas where I knew he had been hurt.

Tigger was still quite weak so she fed him and then wouldn't leave his side, nor he hers.

It was getting dark and nearing the end of another strange but interesting day in the bay, so we decided it was time to leave the pair to re-unite. I then remembered that we hadn't told them all about my brave and successful rescue operation of the alien being. Oh well, that would have to wait until tomorrow as the group was already dispersing in different directions, some to forage for tasty fish, some to rest or play, and others to catch up on news after such unexpected events.

Mum and I, well, we just slept.

15.   The Magic

Hey, guess what — we're in the breakfast room again eating, surprise surprise!

"So that'll be one 'hero's breakfast' coming up then?" smiled Jan, as she piled loads of newspapers onto our table:

Little Girl Saves Dolphin's Life,

Tiny Dolphin Calf Rescues Drowning Boy

and

Cardigan Bay Dolphins - the Heroes of Wales...!

I couldn't believe how many headlines there were about our adventure! I could feel all the other guests looking over and whispering stuff like...

"She and her brother nearly died you know!" and *"Did you know there are magical dolphins living here?!"* said another, and on and on.

Mum said I'd better get used to it as I'm famous now. I just tried to ignore it. All I was interested in was seeing the dolphins again, oh and Jack.

I missed Jack in our little room last night. Poor thing was missing all the excitement being stuck in hospital. The doctors said he would be in for some time 'cos it was a major leg break, so it looked like we would be spending much longer in New Quay than originally planned – oh dear, what a shame ;o)))) YEHOOOOO!!!!!!!!!!!!!!!!!!

Oh crickey, Jan's calling me, wants me to go and see her in the kitchen. Bet it's a telling off for putting Owen's life in danger...here goes.

Well, that was well weird..just had a REALLY heavy talk with Jan... She made me sit down with her at the table. I was nervous but then she took hold of my hands and squeezed them. Straight away I felt better but still had no idea why I was there.

"The biologists would like to see you at their office this morning, sweetheart, if you're free?" she smiled. "Really? Why?" I asked. "Well, because you saved a precious dolphin's life, I should think!" laughed Jan, smiling at me.

She told me I'm special and that she'd spotted it as soon as she saw me. She had seen it once before with someone who came to visit the dolphins, but has never seen it again.. Then she looked right in to my eyes and said, "I know you've seen the magic, Lucy. I know you've experienced it. You are so lucky. Lots of folk would have missed it. Wouldn't have seen it coming and would have let it pass them by. But you,

you saw it and because of that, you will ALWAYS have it. It will never leave you now, unless of course you ignore it. Once you ignore the magic and close your mind to what you are shown you will never ever be shown again."

"I don't know if it's the dolphins that pick the ones to receive the magic or if it's someone or something else that decides, but I do know that what you did yesterday was an exceptional thing, and although I don't agree that children go off in the dead of night and risk their lives, I still believe that there was only one person who had the courage to go ahead and save that special little dolphin...and that person was you."

I was ~~flobber-garsted~~ flabbergasted and not sure what to say. Which question out of the hundreds that were flying around in my head should I ask first? But I ran out of time because, just at that moment, a strong smell of fish wafted into the kitchen, followed by Owen.

"Ah, it's our little 'Dolphin Defender!'" he said brightly. At that very moment I totally understood what I would be when I grew up. It was all so clear to me. All those thoughts and feelings I'd had for many years about animals and their safety. All those questions I had about nature, and the creatures that lived alongside us.

"Now, go and get yourself off to the scientists' office and find out how you can help each other" said Jan, squeezing my hands, and with eyes full of encouragement, "Our oceans are a magnificent and precious place and need protecting, and you have a long career ahead of you doing just that. After all, you've made an excellent start!"

After visiting the group of scientists, we went to see Jack. I was so excited and could hardly wait to tell him my fab-tab-ulous news.

I burst through the waiting room and straight into his ward, running towards his bed where he lay with his leg pointed up towards the ceiling, covered in white plaster.

"Jack! Jack! Guess what? The dolphin researchers want me to spend the rest of the summer with them learning all about the dolphins, and how to study and look after them, isn't it wicked Jack!"

He looked as chuffed as I felt and said he always knew I'd do something amazing...aww ;o))

"And you Jack, how are you feeling today?" asked Dad,
"Great!" he said, with a HUGE cheesy grin all over his face.
We couldn't really figure out what he was so happy about...
"I've decided that when I'm older, I'm going to work for the coastguard with a search and rescue team!"

Yikes, you should have seen Mum's face! Looks like the magic in Cardigan Bay has got to both of us!

16. Time to move on

So the buzz going around the group was that we would be leaving any day now. The fish were becoming harder to find, the seas were changing due to the weather, and Tigger was becoming stronger and stronger. We would be departing as a group, heading further north for the winter, where more plentiful fish stocks swam. I was looking forward to the journey, the companionship, and the experience of discovering a new place outside of the bay. Although I would miss this place that had been my home for the past six months, we would be returning in the spring, Mum told me. I didn't know what the spring was but it sounded good anyway, and just the fact that we would be returning pleased me no end.

So this was my first season in Cardigan Bay. I had been born, made life-long friends, learned how to be a dolphin calf, I had drunk lots of milk, played many great games, learned how to swim, jump, leap, communicate, and detect things with my sonar ability, and I had helped save my best friend's life, and, to top it all, saved the life of an alien being. Not bad for such a little dolphin.

I had also learned that the bay was relatively safe for dolphins, safer than most other waters I'd heard about, but that there would always be risks and dangers lurking around corners. However, so long as I was wise, remembered the new skills I'd learned, and stuck close to Mum, I should be fine.

I hadn't really understood what 'safe' had meant during those very early days. I was having such a blast that nothing else really mattered, but now I thought I knew, well a little anyway. I had learned so much in these first six months.

The day that was chosen for our move was bright and sunny, and all of us seemed in high spirits and keen for the journey to begin. As we travelled, we passed some of the very shallow areas of the bay that I knew well, where many times I had watched the sun send out little patterns onto the sandy bottom, which I loved to chase and scatter about by flicking up the grains with my beak. I could feel an energy passing all through the group, an excitement and a feeling of what was to come. It was infectious. I soon became highly excitable and Mum had to tell me to calm down, but I loved it. I loved being part of such a large group, watching the stronger

males and the feeling of sticking together and bonding. We were heading out of my home area, the area I knew well, and into unknown territory. The pace was picking up as we swam on, strong in our unison. Surfacing for quick breaths, then swooping back down to glide along using flicks of our tails, and then a further flick would send us down and flying along the ocean floor. I felt free, free as a dolphin.

We were making good progress and, so far, none of us needed to rest, not even Tigger. The sea had become darker and felt colder, and the cliffs that lined our route were larger and more rugged. As I leaped and jumped through the choppy top layer of water, I could see the air-world landscape was certainly different to the sheltered bay.

It wasn't long before a loud series of clicks were heard from the front of our group. I wasn't sure what was going on but all the adults seemed to pick up their pace, swooping and flying around. It was like being in the middle of a whirlwind.

"*Over here!*" clicked Splash, as he launched himself wonderfully out of the water, and landed with hardly a ripple as his dorsal fin cut finely past my beak. One strong flick of his tail and he sent something flying through the air, towards one of his friends who swooped underneath the object and sent it flying in the opposite direction. This time I saw it land nearby only to be launched high up in the air for a third time, and out of my reach.

I found out it was a jellyfish, and there were many more of them being flicked skilfully around to different members of the group. What a wonderful way to say goodbye to the bay, by playing one of a dolphin's absolutely favourite games…jelly-ball.

It was my turn to flick the jelly, so with all my strength and determination I slid underneath it, lined up my flukes with the oncoming wobbly ball, and flicked as hard as I could. We all watched as it went spinning high into the air, tentacles flailing around. Those poor unsuspecting jellyfish didn't stand a chance. Still, we made sure we didn't antagonise them for too long, and that we were sure not to cause them any harm.

They did make for fabulous launching objects, though. I'll definitely remember that game for the future!

But where was Mum…? Mum seemed to have separated herself from the rest of the group. I could see her busying herself on the seabed some distance away, which had changed from a sandy surface to a rocky one. I swam down to where she was, curious to see what was keeping her so entertained. She was using her sonar and clicking furiously at a large cluster of rocks, turning herself upside down and forcing her beak into a tiny hole. What was she doing?

Suddenly, the shiny glint of an eye caught my attention. Mum lunged forward and tried to grab the creature, but, as she did so, it retreated back into the rock. Mum swam with such speed to the other side of the rock, buzzing and clicking it with such force that the poor creature which was trying its best to remain undetected inside, had become so panicked and confused with all the vibrations that it backed out of its hiding place just a little too far.

With the ease and swiftness that only a dolphin possesses, Mum easily snatched the poor creature in her beak and shot up to the surface with it.

Mum had caught one of a dolphin's most highly prized suppers, and she knew it.

There she was, with the conger eel between her teeth, flicking it around and showing it off to the others with a look on her face that told them all,

'There you go, look at me, the dolphin that got the conger.'

"You keep following in her wake, and you'll go far" clicked a voice from behind, *"I know you were the one who saved that alien being"* it continued. I recognised the clicks immediately and turned to see my dad. *"Wanna know the real reason why you got your name?"* he clicked again. I nodded. *"Cos you're bright, 'as bright as a button'"*, and giving my fin a friendly little nibble he then swam up from beneath me and lifted me high into the sky.

Being lifted up onto my dad's back, it suddenly dawned on me that a dolphin's world was huge - enormous in fact, and there was so much to learn and accomplish before I would be independent and capable of looking after myself. The adventures I'd been involved in so far, although dramatic, were a mere drop in a dolphin's ocean, and I must be wise and use the wit I had been born with to survive.

If I was, as my dad had said, bright as a button, I might stand a chance.

And so we travelled on northwards, Mum, Dad and me, and the rest of the gang - the sun setting beyond a little island, but with an exciting new season awaiting us.

I'm nearly at the end of my story. But not quite...

Obviously, I joined the scientists for the last weeks of the summer and worked as hard as hard can be. I learned about the ocean, the animals that live in it, and all about the bottlenose dolphins of Cardigan Bay. But, more importantly, I learned how I can help to protect the ocean and the animals whose lives depend on it. I also discovered that every decision and every action that a human being makes, has knock-on effects on the environment.

I sat on the quay every single day, counting and recording the dolphins. I saw Tigger, the little calf that had been entangled in the ghost netting that had been so carelessly thrown from someone's boat into the ocean, and watched it grow stronger and saw how its scars began to heal.

The scientists asked me to officially name Nic Nic's calf and I told them that I already had, on the very first day of my holiday, when I first met him!

Button and Nic Nic visited me at the quay every day and hung around for a long time whistling to me, then one day I didn't see them anymore. At first I was upset and worried, but then someone explained that a large pod of bottlenose dolphins had been seen heading northwards out of the bay earlier that day, but would be returning in the spring. I was going to miss them so much!

The hard working researchers, who had taught me so much, said that I could join them any time and that I was a huge asset to their team! Can you believe it...me being good at something! So I decided on the spot that I too would return to Cardigan Bay in the spring.

I continued to have the dreams and magical experiences, but I didn't see them as strange anymore. I knew it was Stripey, the magic dolphin. He was protecting the pod and teaching me that there was heaps of work to be done to protect the oceans and to keep them a safe environment for dolphins and other animals to live in happily, and it was *my* job to make sure it was done!

Oh, and one last thing, I got an A✩✩✩ for this diary (10/10), just as I'd hoped I would ;o))))

The End of my Dolphin Diary
By Lucy Hensure, aged 8.

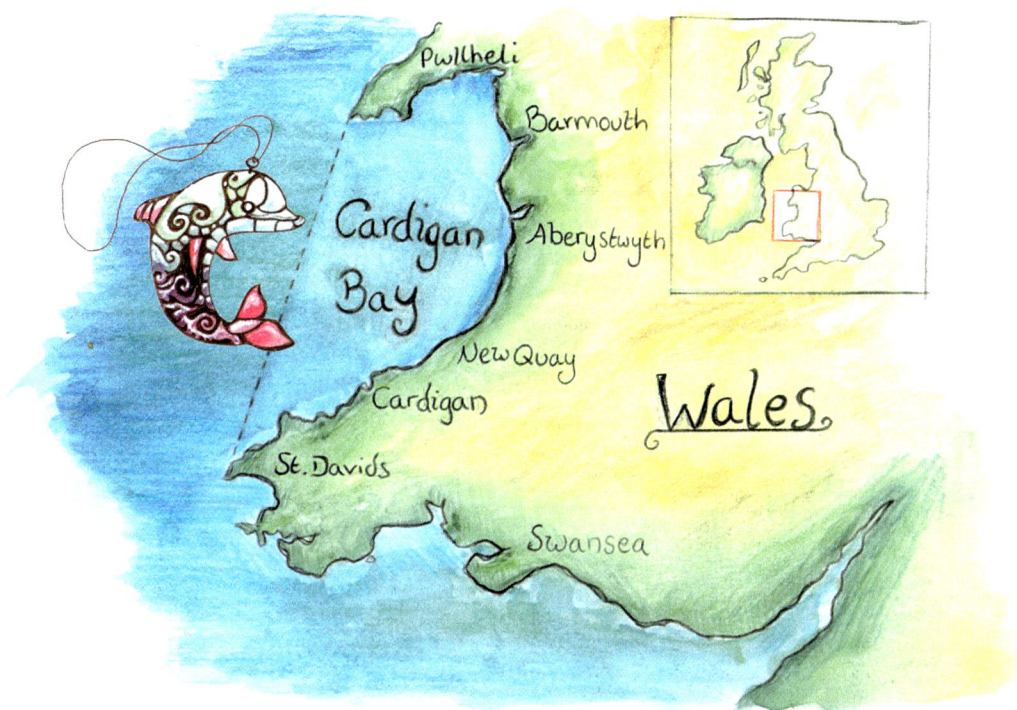

Pwllheli

Barmouth

Aberystwyth

Cardigan
Bay

New Quay

Cardigan

Wales

St. Davids

Swansea

The Bottlenose Dolphin Family Tree

Can you figure out who is related to whom?

Answers: Rip Torn & Nic Nic have had two calves Button & Splash. Bond & Chris had Tigger. Tide & Smoothy had Lumpy. And Gandalf & Topnotch had Coral.

SCIENTIFIC NOTE ABOUT THE DOLPHINS

Button, Tigger and all the dolphins named in this book are real dolphins, and their names are the real names we give them in our scientific research. Around two hundred dolphins live in the vicinity of Cardigan Bay in West Wales, making it the largest bottlenose dolphin community in all the coastal waters of the British Isles. We have been studying them here for more than a decade, working on behalf of the Welsh Government's conservation body, Natural Resources Wales.

All the photographs in this book were taken in Wales during the course of our research. We can recognise individual dolphins by the nicks and marks on their fins and back, most having a unique pattern. That is how we can name them and be confident of being able to track them through their lifetime. Bottlenose dolphins can live for many years. Animals that are fifty years old have been recorded in other parts of the world where they have been studied a long time. In many cases they are likely to out-live the career of an individual researcher. However, just like Tigger found out, the first few years of life in particular can be perilous. In Cardigan Bay we have found that one fifth of all calves born die in their first year, and more than half will be dead by the time they are three years old. We don't always know the cause of death but the two greatest threats that we have identified are human disturbance from pleasure craft and entanglement in fishing gear.

In Europe the most important piece of conservation legislation aimed at protecting our wildlife is the Habitats Directive. Bottlenose dolphins are recognised as at particular risk from human activities by the fact that they often occur in coastal waters where such activities are greatest – industrial development, pollution, fishing, shipping and recreation all occur particularly in these regions. For this reason the species is given special protection by law in the form of a network of marine protected areas called Special Areas of Conservation. In the British Isles, there are three such areas to protect the bottlenose dolphin. Two of these are in Wales, in Cardigan Bay, and the third is in the Moray Firth in North-east Scotland where another important bottlenose dolphin community lives.

The names of the two bottlenose dolphin Special Areas of Conservation (called SACs for short) in Wales are Pen Llyn a'r Sarnau around the Llyn Peninsula that forms the northern boundary of Cardigan Bay, and one called Cardigan Bay SAC in the southern part of the bay. Button was born in this latter region quite close to the little town of New Quay. Although many dolphins live within the Bay, and are born there, they don't all remain there through their lives. In fact most of the population migrate out of the Bay in the autumn and spend the winter months roaming the high seas off North Wales reaching as far as the Isle of Man and beyond. Here, they face all sorts of other dangers but also other opportunities – different kinds of fish, which can form concentrations for example when spawning. In those situations, the fish make a welcome tasty meal for the dolphins which otherwise have to brave the winter storms.

We study the dolphins using many different techniques – observing and counting them from land, going out in boats to survey and photograph them, and deploying hydrophones and other detectors that record their voices – whistles or clicks. Working from a research office in New Quay, Sea Watch staff and volunteers every summer conduct this research. Then during the cold winter months, they concentrate upon analysing and writing up the results. These studies provide us with the scientific information we need to help manage and protect the dolphins.

You can contribute to care for the bottlenose dolphins of Cardigan Bay by adopting one of them, and follow its fortunes and those of its companions, through our Adopt a Dolphin scheme. Full details can be found at www.adoptadolphin.org.uk or on the Sea Watch website www.seawatchfoundation.org.uk. You could also come to Cardigan Bay and go out on a boat to see the dolphins, and by all means visit us at our Welsh office – Paragon House, Wellington Place, New Quay, Ceredigion SA45 9NR.

Dr Peter Evans
Director
Sea Watch Foundation

BIOGRAPHIES

Kirsten Hintner has had a varied career as writer, filmmaker and producer, working for a variety of bodies including the BBC and Open University, and subsequently running her own company. Kirsten has several years experience working with children and young adults on filming projects and various educational enterprises. In 2010, she ran a series of environmental filming workshops for schools in Pembrokeshire, the two film products winning first and second prizes in their respective categories at a National Schools Media Awards Ceremony in 2011. She is the Administrator of Sea Watch's Adopt A Dolphin scheme, editing also its newsletters. She has had a passion for conservation and the welfare of animals and wildlife since a very young child, and her aim is to make a difference within the world of conservation and welfare, and to help protect animals and threatened species internationally.
www.kirstenhintner.co.uk
www.creativeconservation.co.uk

Dr Peter Evans is Director of the UK marine environmental research charity, Sea Watch Foundation, and an Honorary Senior Lecturer in the School of Ocean Sciences, University of Wales Bangor. An international authority on marine mammals, he advises the European Commission, national governments, industry, and conservation NGOs on cetaceans. He was founding Secretary and later Chairman of the European Cetacean Society, and edited *European Research on Cetaceans* for twenty years. A member of the Advisory Committee of the international conservation agreement ASCOBANS, he was given the Education and Outreach Award by UNEP in 2009; and in 2012, the European Cetacean Society gave him the award for outstanding contribution to marine mammal conservation. He has given more than 100 talks at international conferences and symposia in 25 countries, written or edited 12 books, and is sole or co-author of about 200 scientific publications. He is a keen amateur photographer and has won awards for his photographs of marine wildlife.

Credits Most of the photographs in this book were taken by Peter Evans. Pia Anderwald is particularly acknowledged for kindly allowing use of her excellent images (Pp. 13, 25, 31, 72, 85, 100, 107, 108), as also are Mick Baines (P.21 top), Ronnie Dyer (P. 73), Daphna Feingold (P. 30), Teo Leyssen (P. 74), Mandy McMath (P. 10), Giovanna Pesante (Pp. 24, 38, 81 top), and Christopher Swann (P. 12). Melanie Broadhurst produced the map (P.16), Paul Daley drew the crab (P26), and Alice Ormiston did a tremendous job producing all the other illustrations.

Kirsten's next book…

Patched-Up

Patch, a scruffy, lovable lurcher is born and grows up in a traveller's camp and all is well, until things begin to change and life takes a frightening and unpredictable turn. Time to escape! However, Patch's adventures lead him into yet more danger. Sadly, he becomes badly injured and has to learn to cope with being disabled. But all is not lost - when nine-year old Timothy, who struggles with disability himself, falls head over heels for Patch…life takes yet another turn.

'Patched-Up' is a moving tale with a strong message of what's right and wrong when it comes to how we treat our animal relatives.

A story for all animal lovers.

For more information visit www.creativeconservation.co.uk